Cars Trucks Planes Helicopter Boats Coloring book: for Kids Toddler Preschool

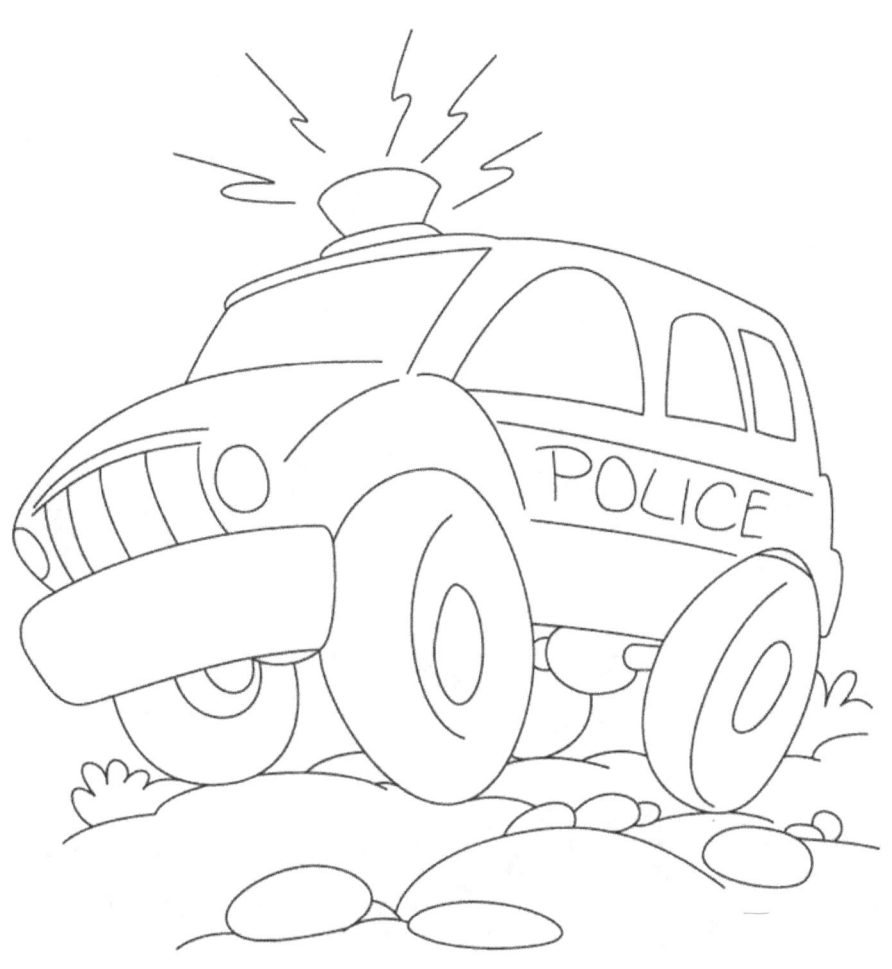

Nina Packer

Coloring book
For Boys , Toddler , Preschool,

Copyright: Published in the United States Nina Packer
Published December 2017

ISBN-13: 978-1982020507

ISBN-10: 1982020504

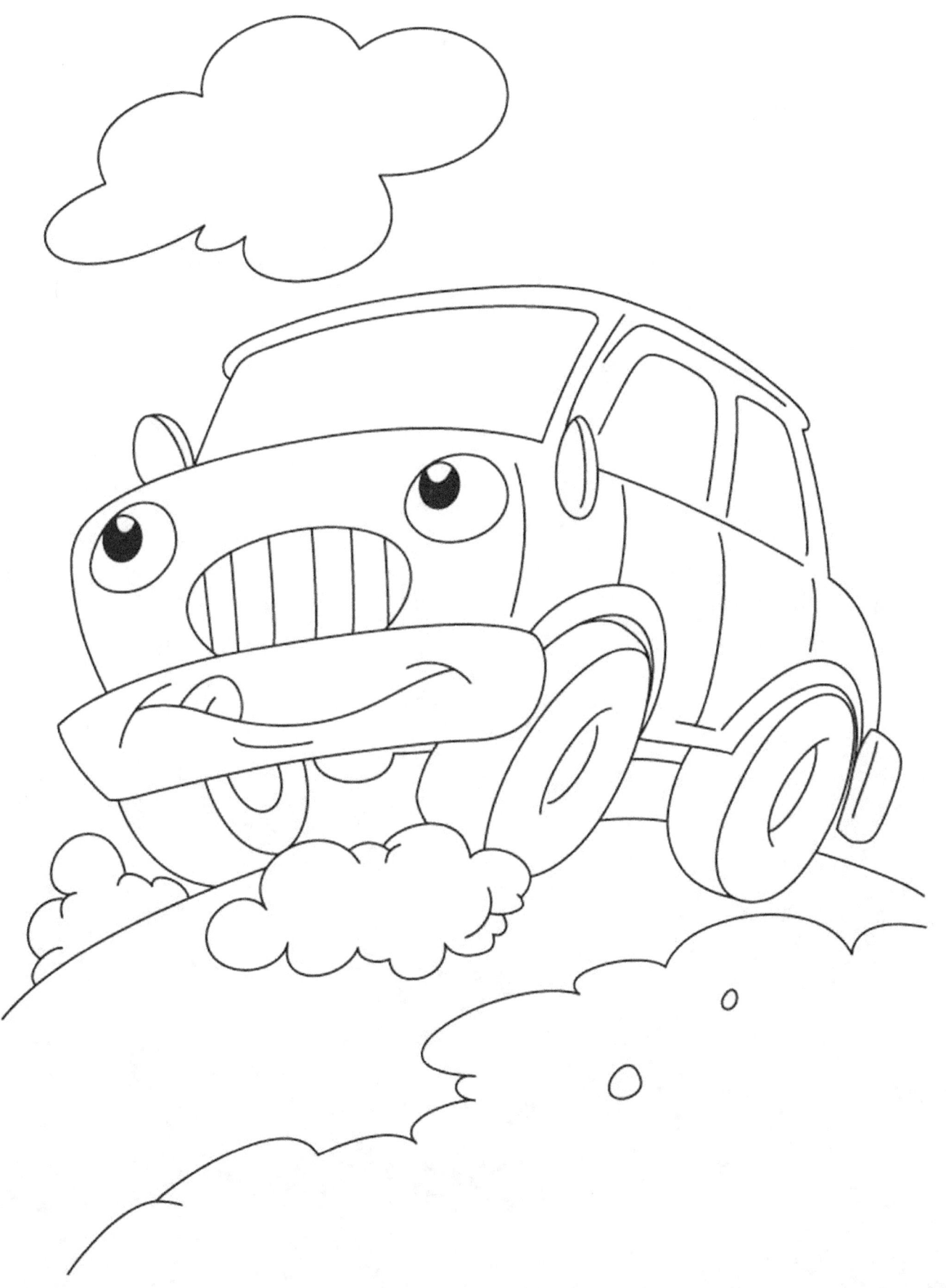

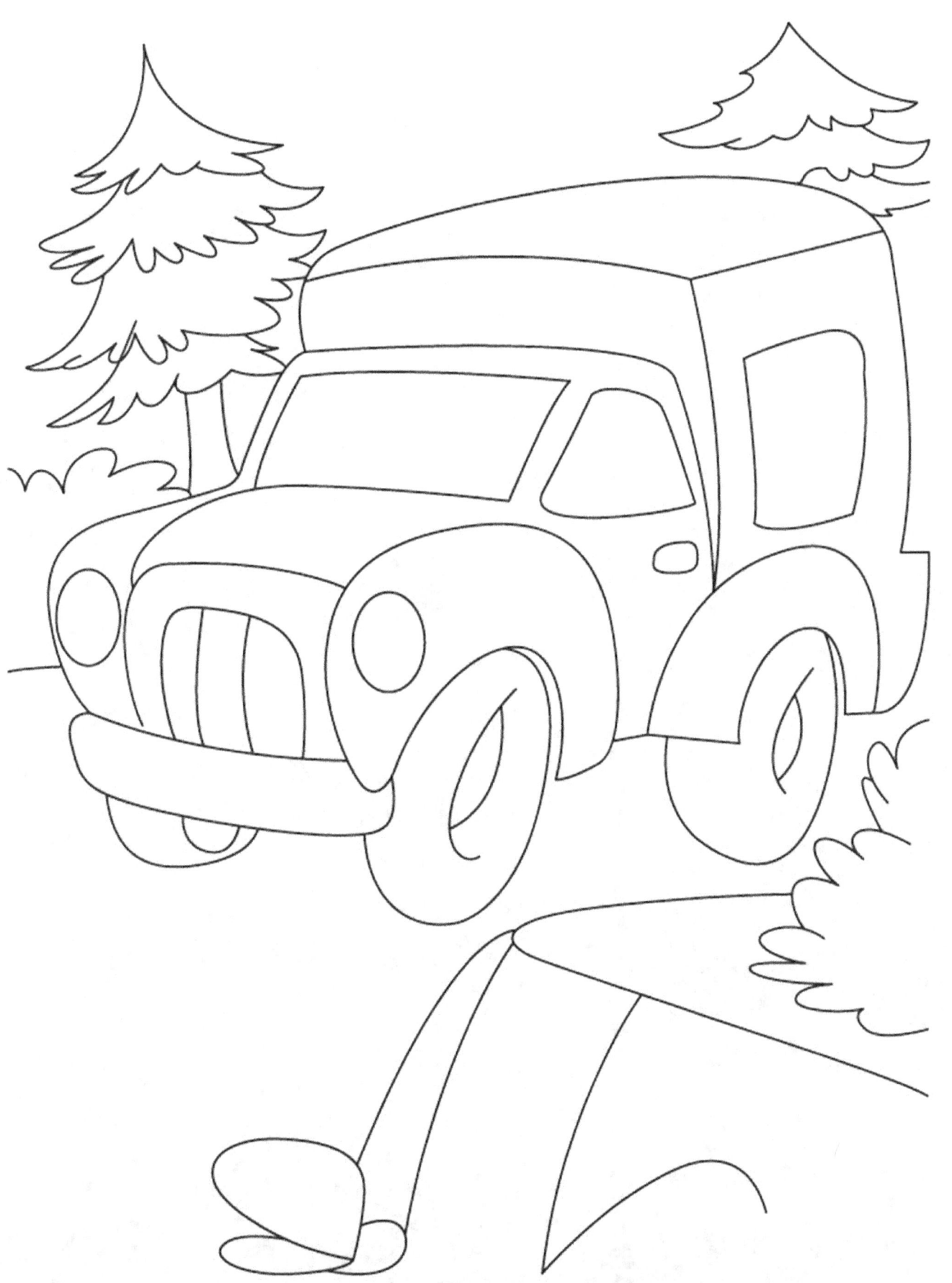

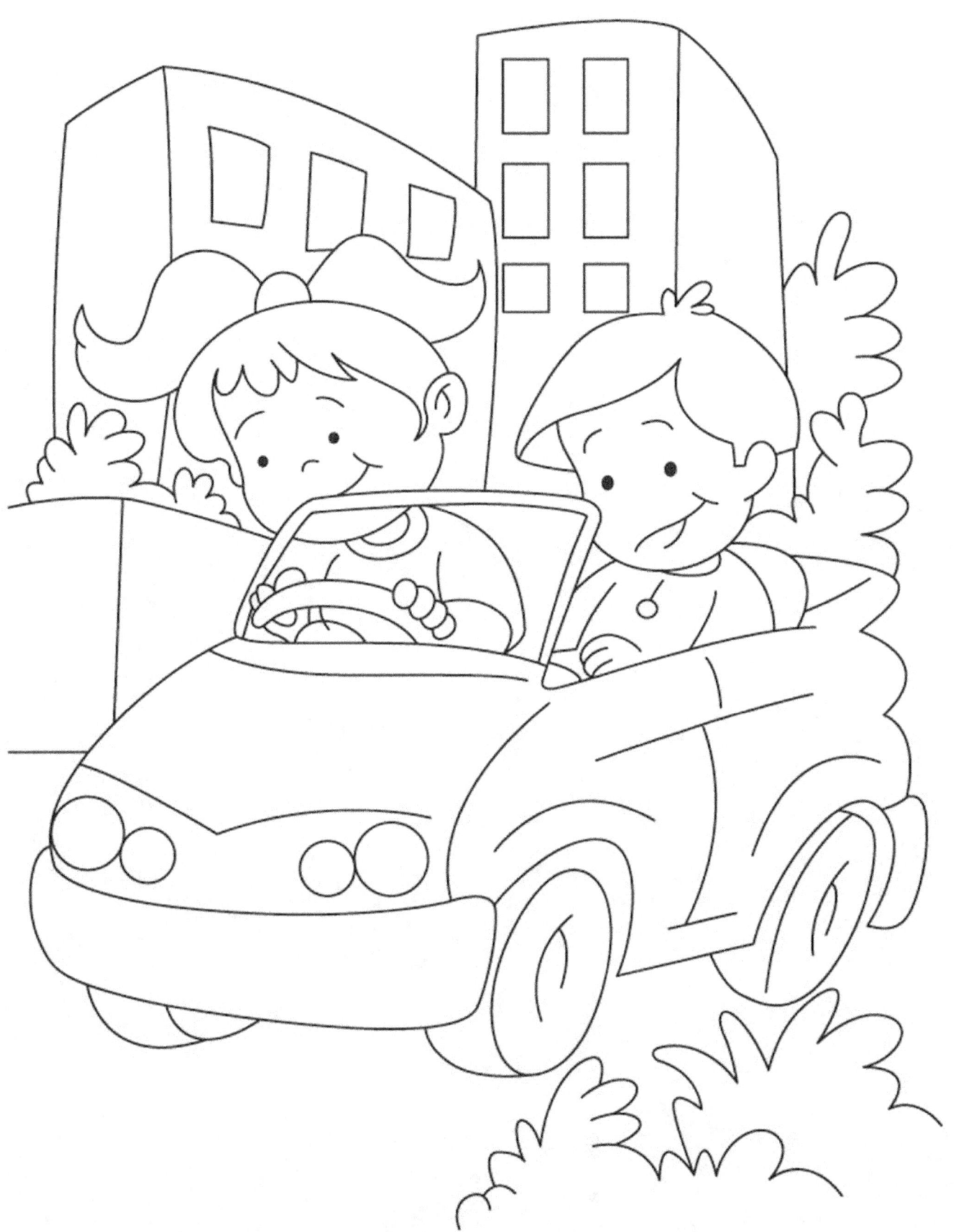

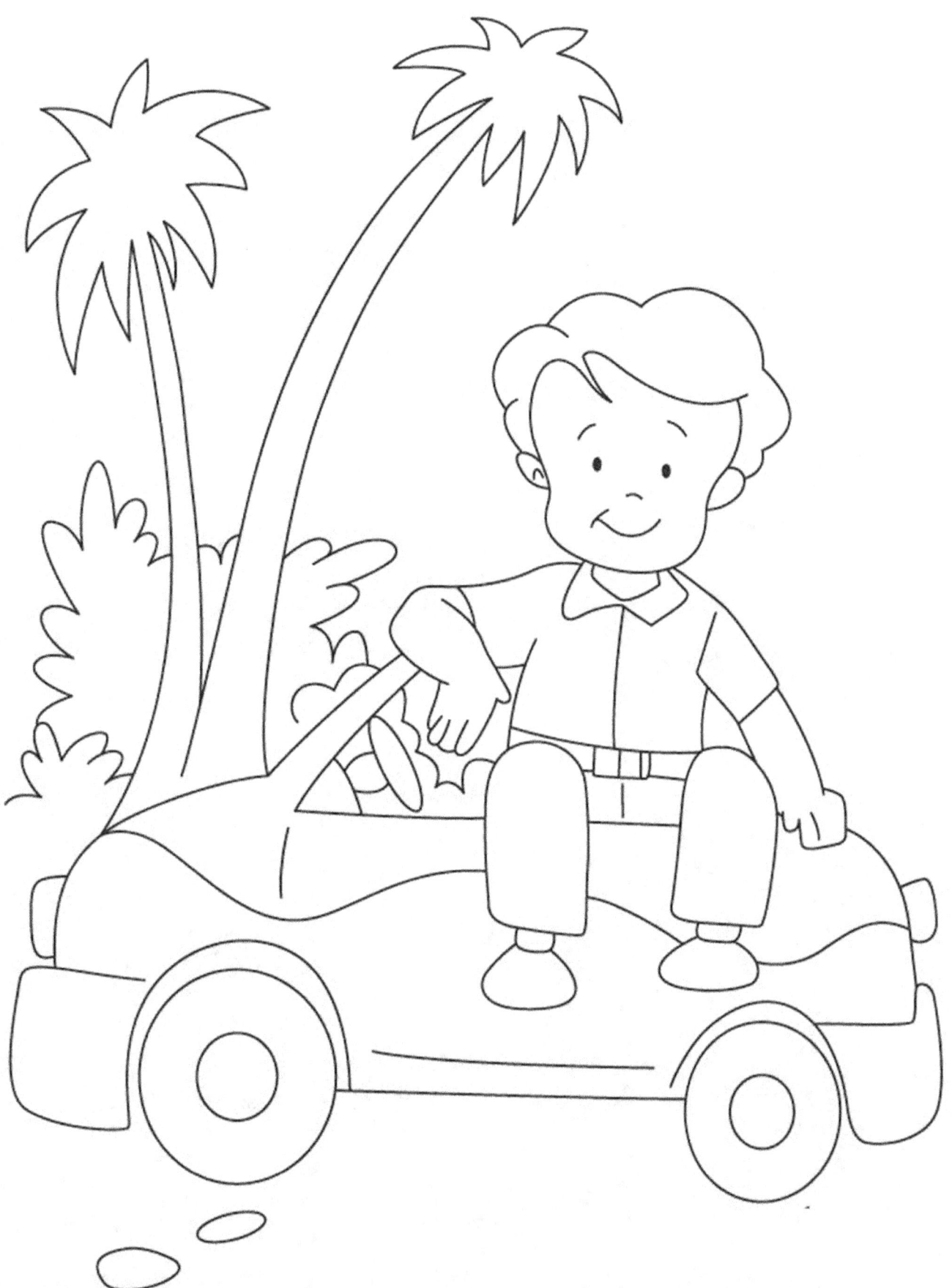

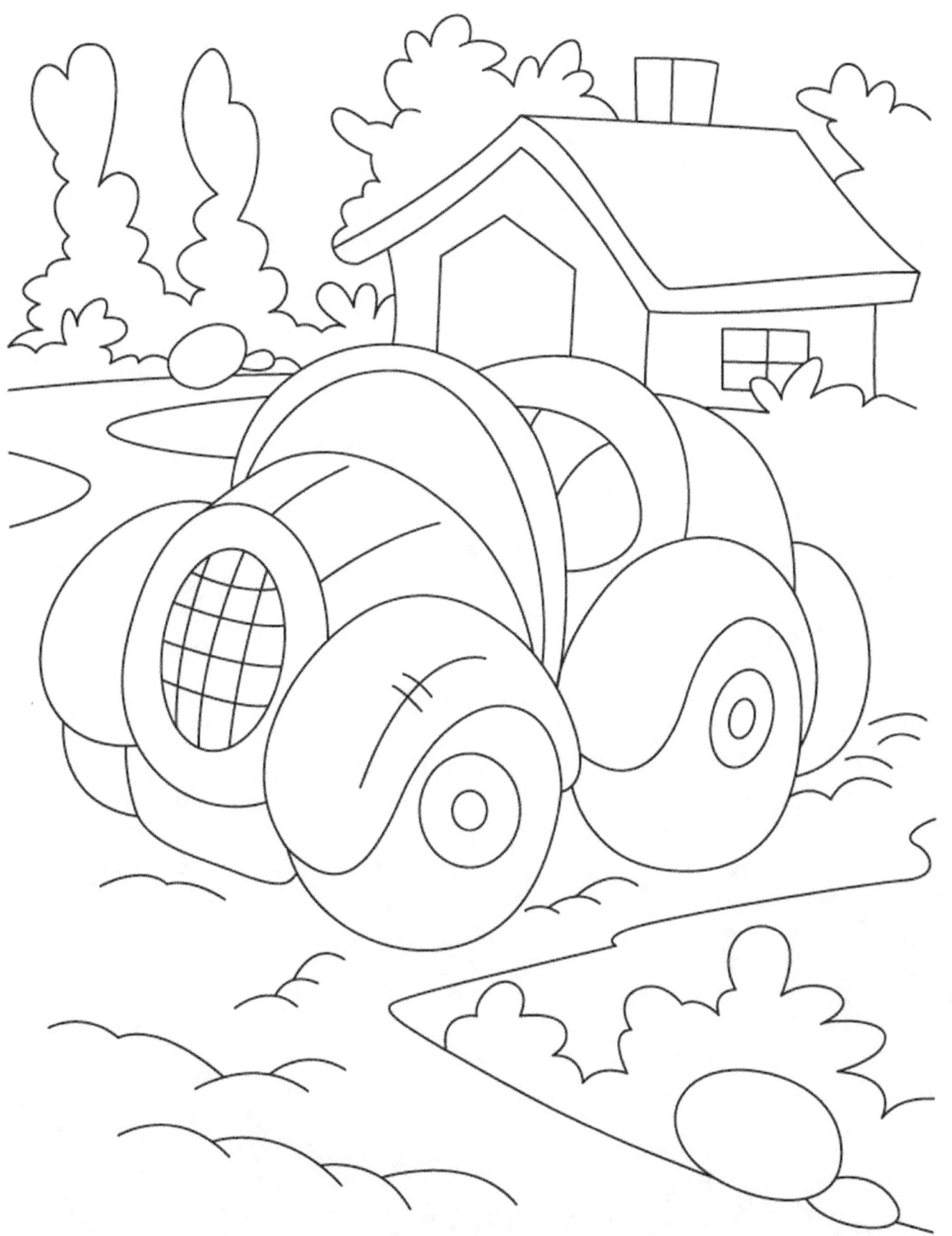

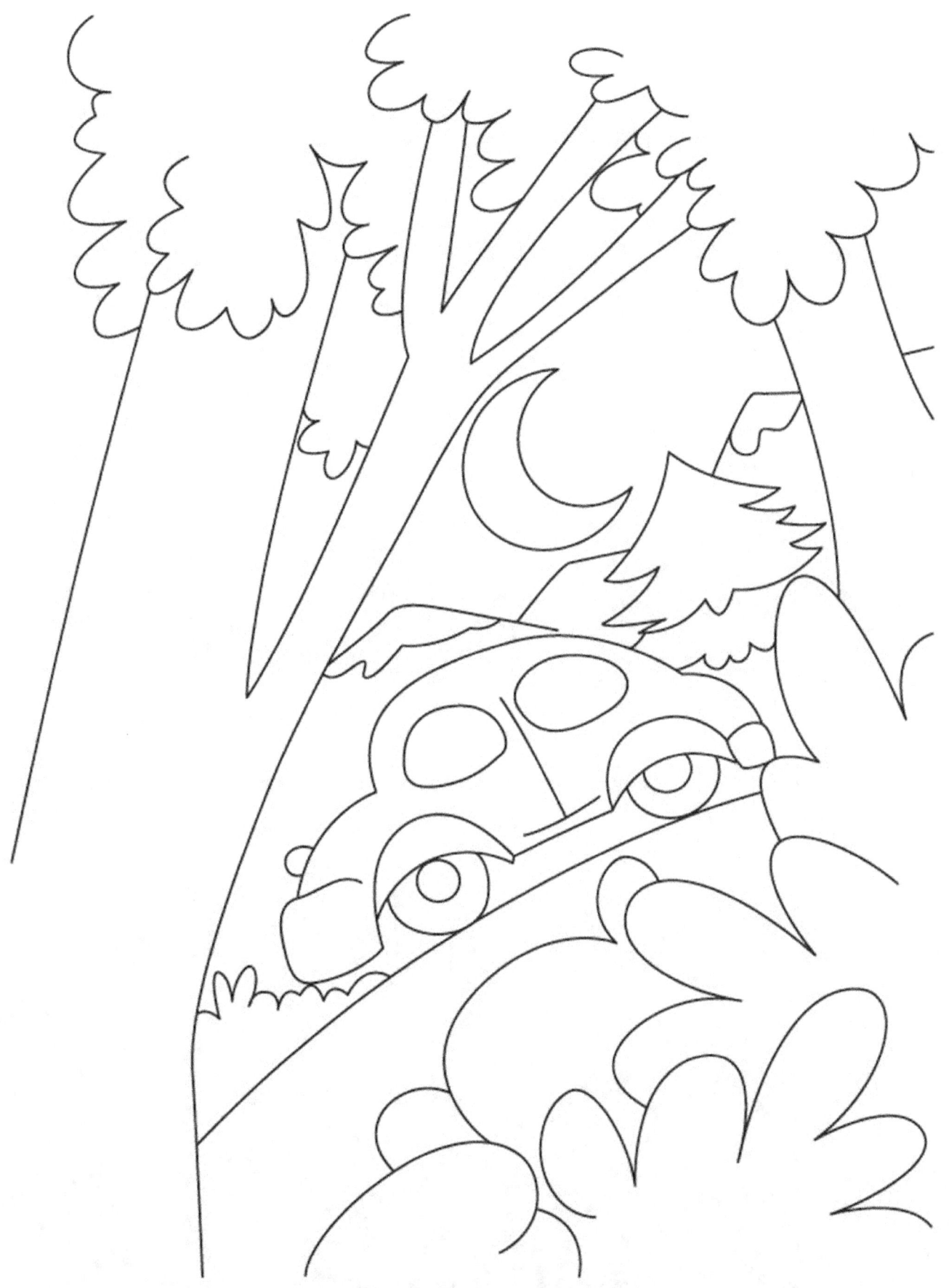

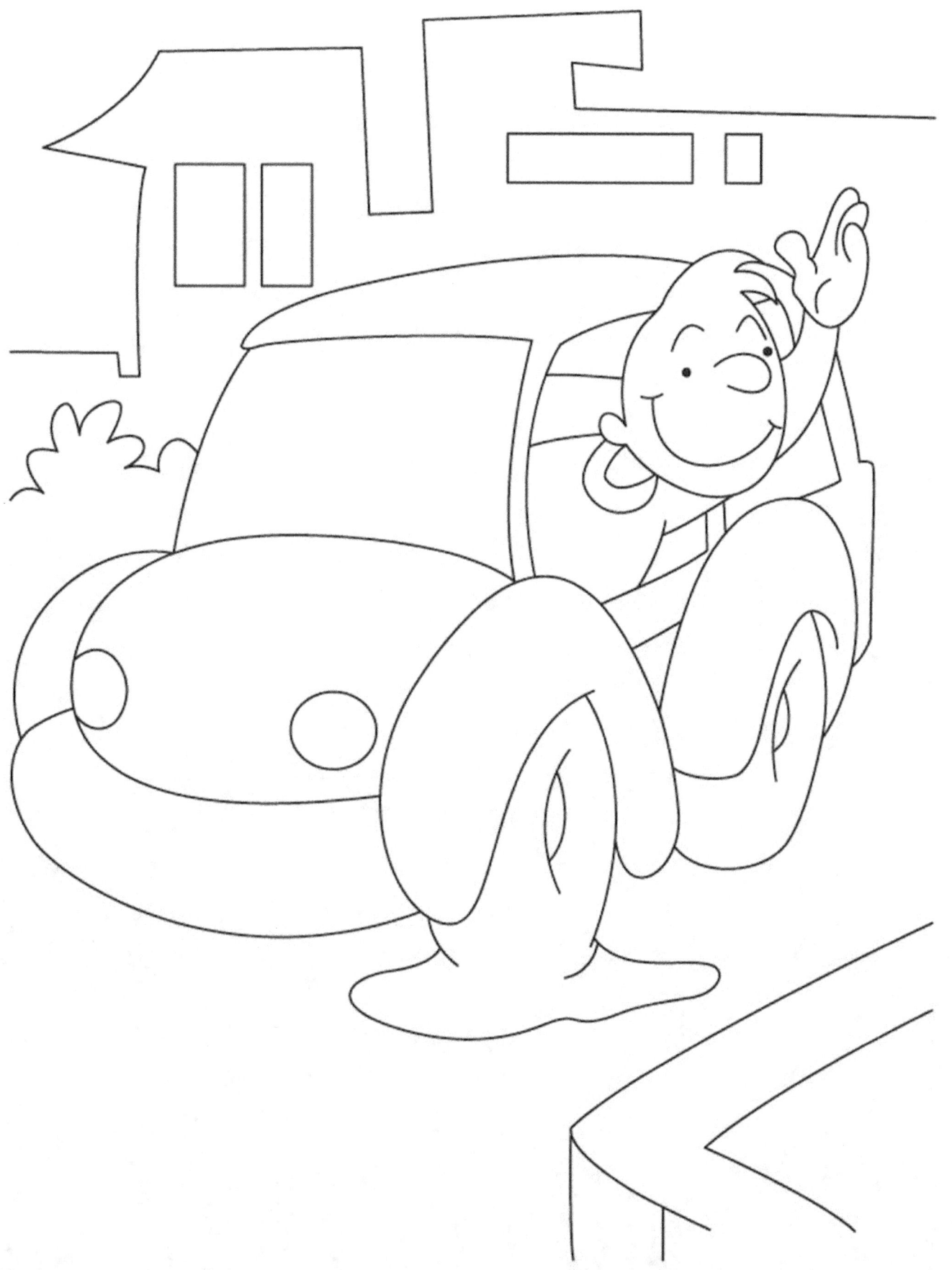

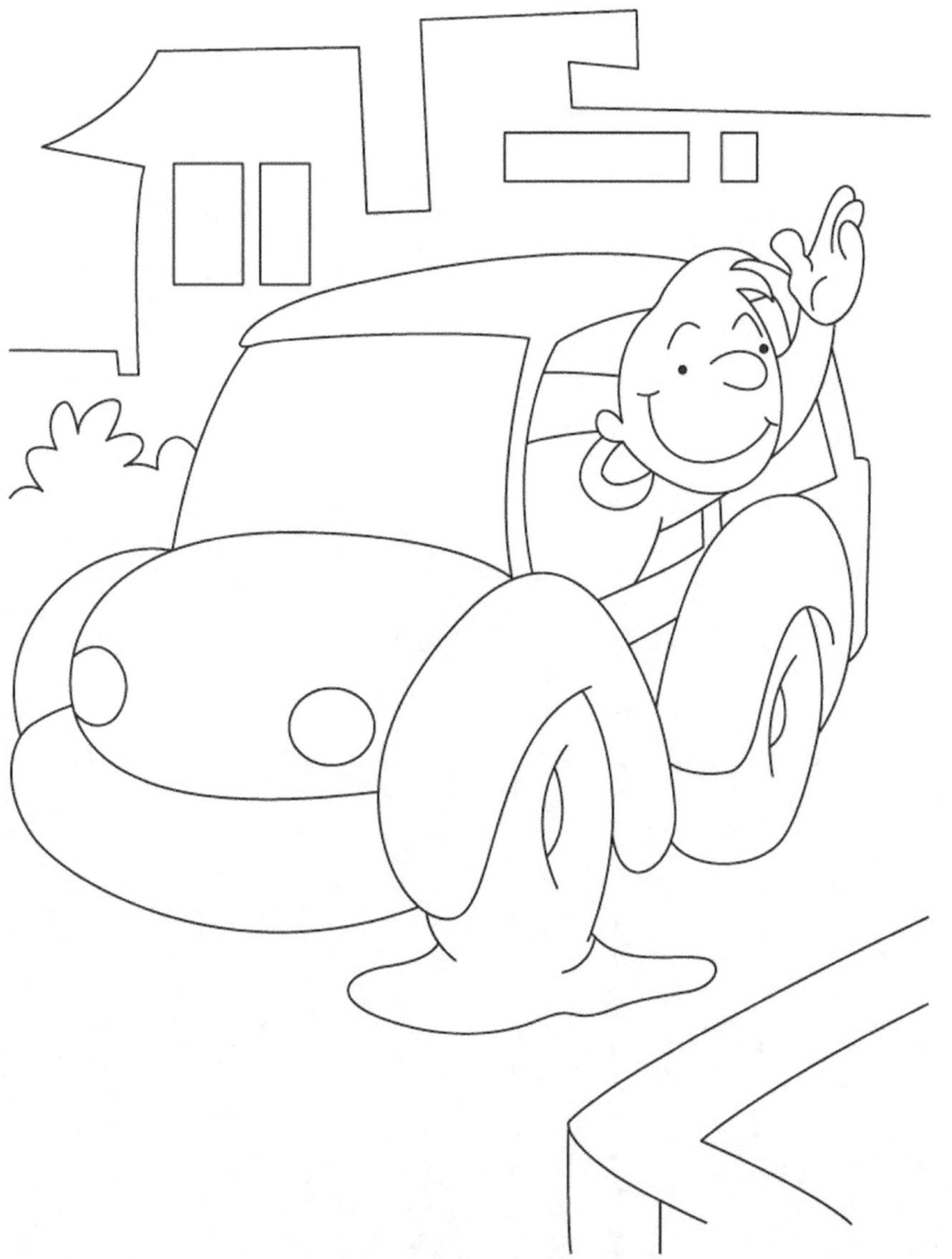

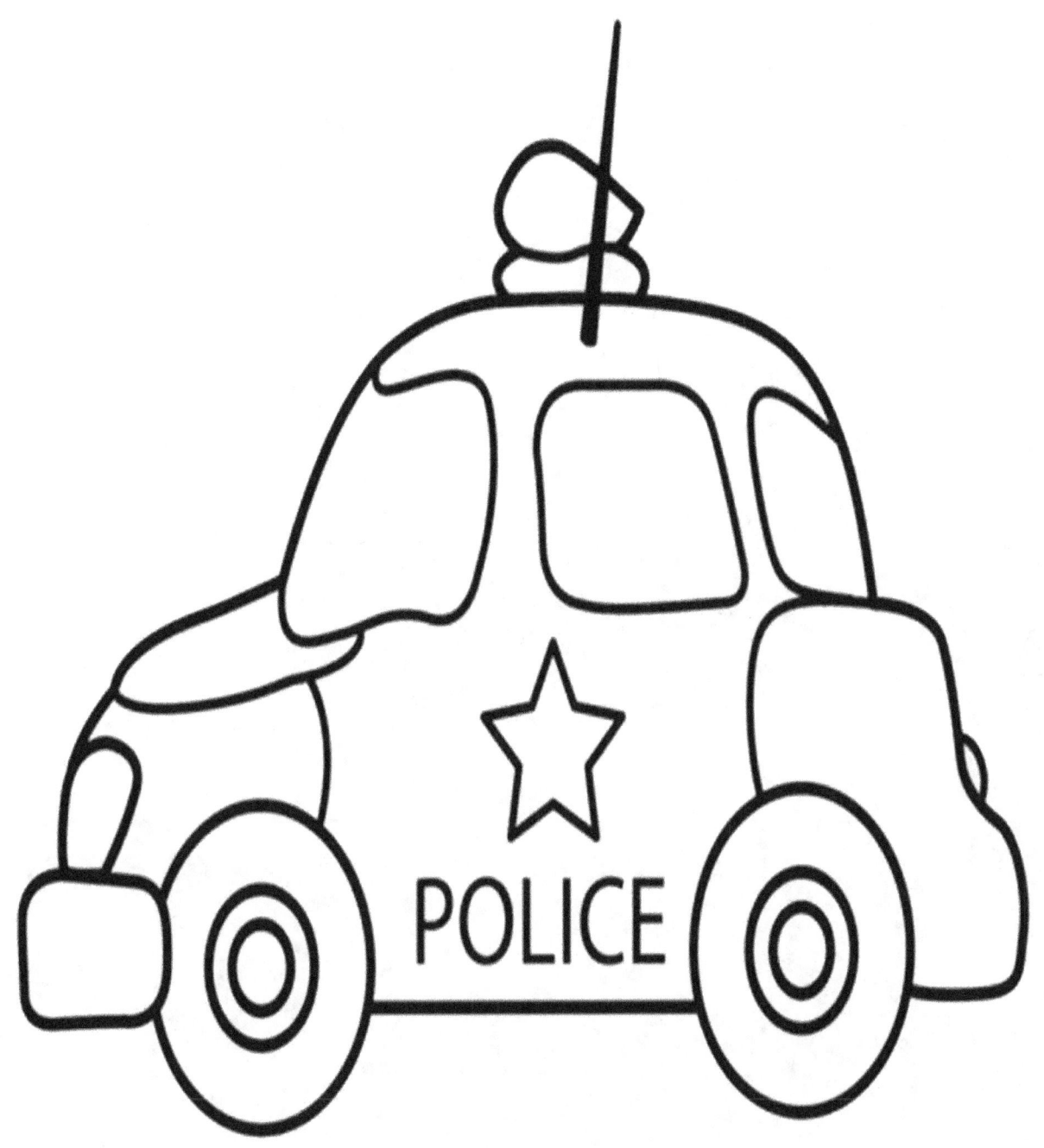

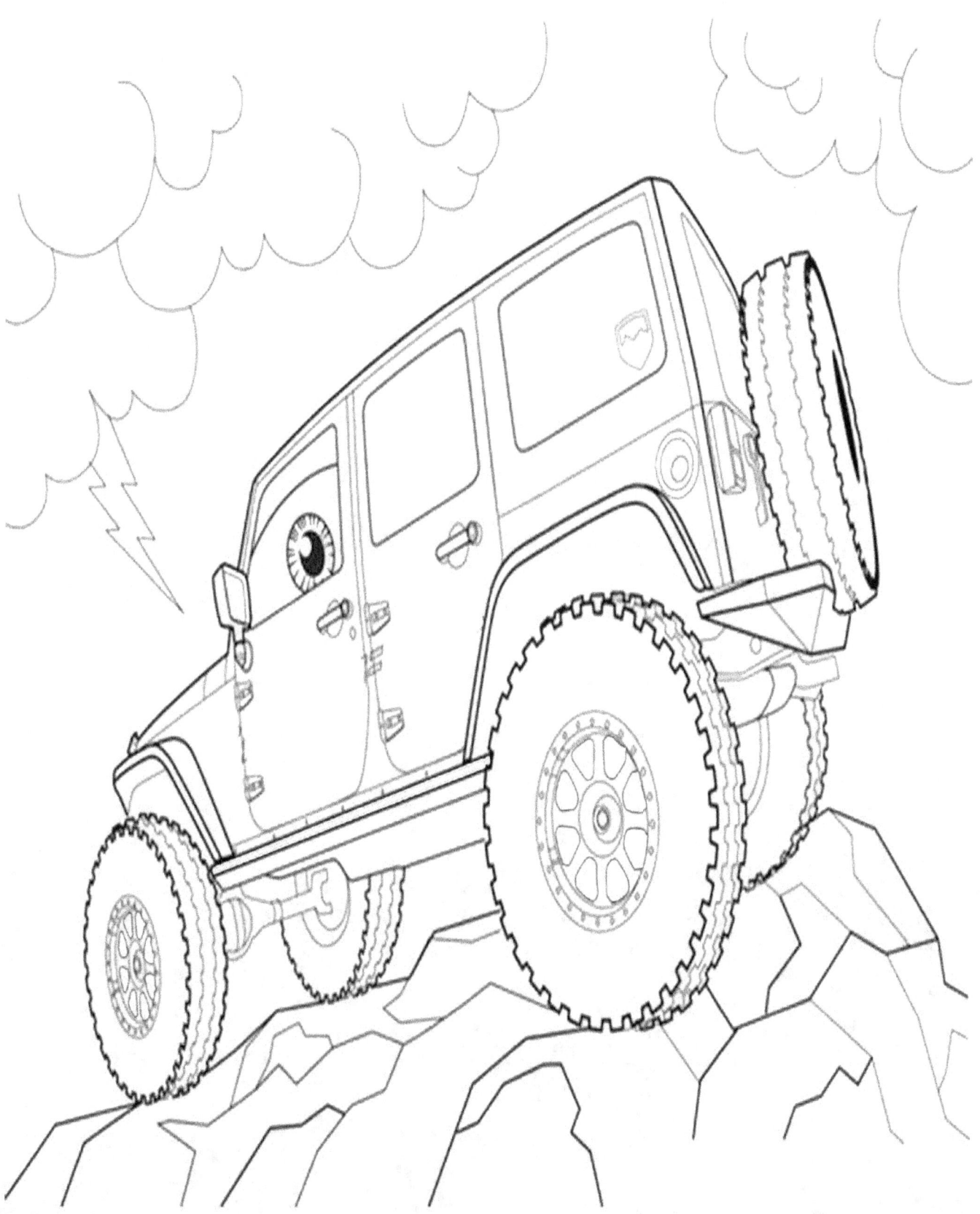

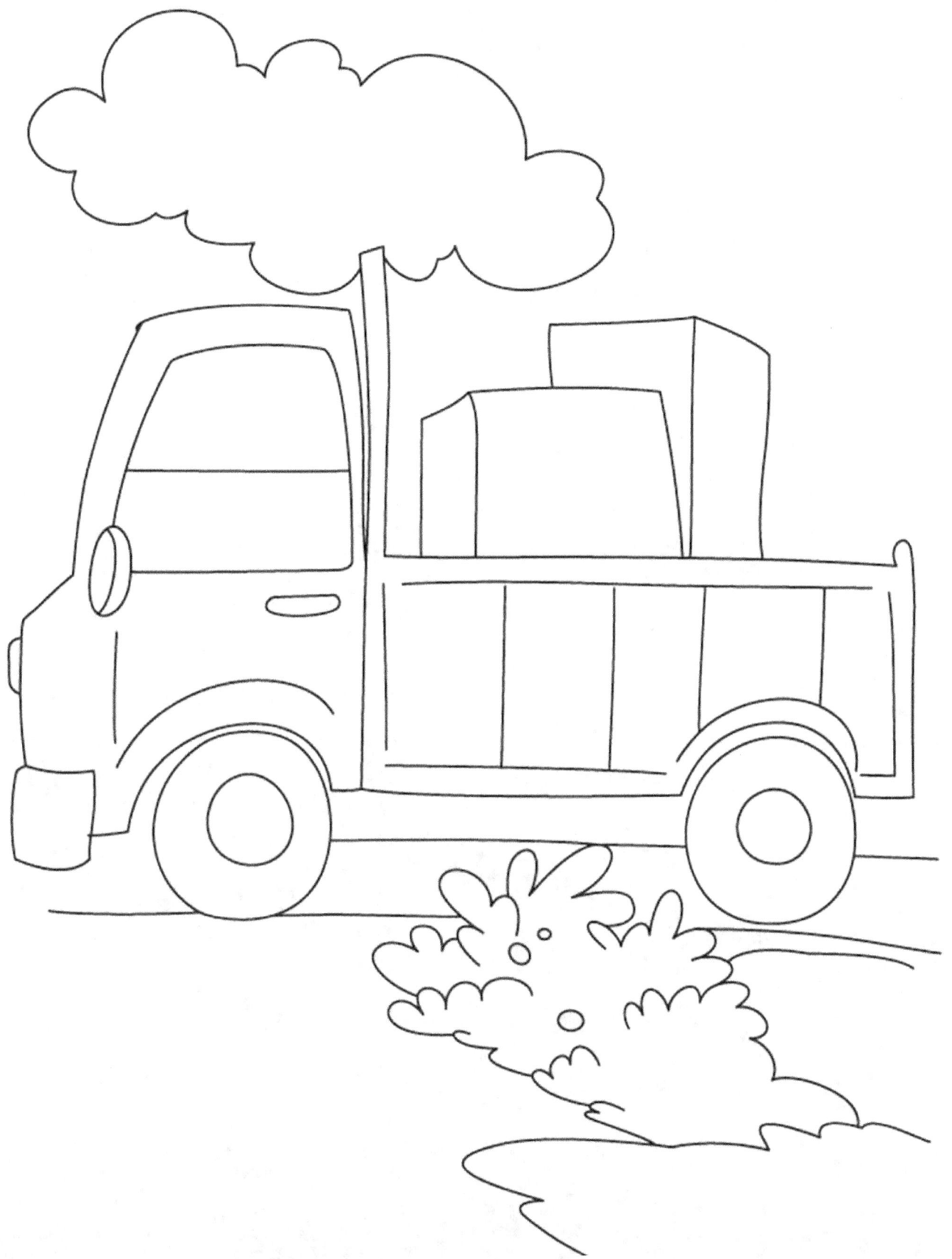

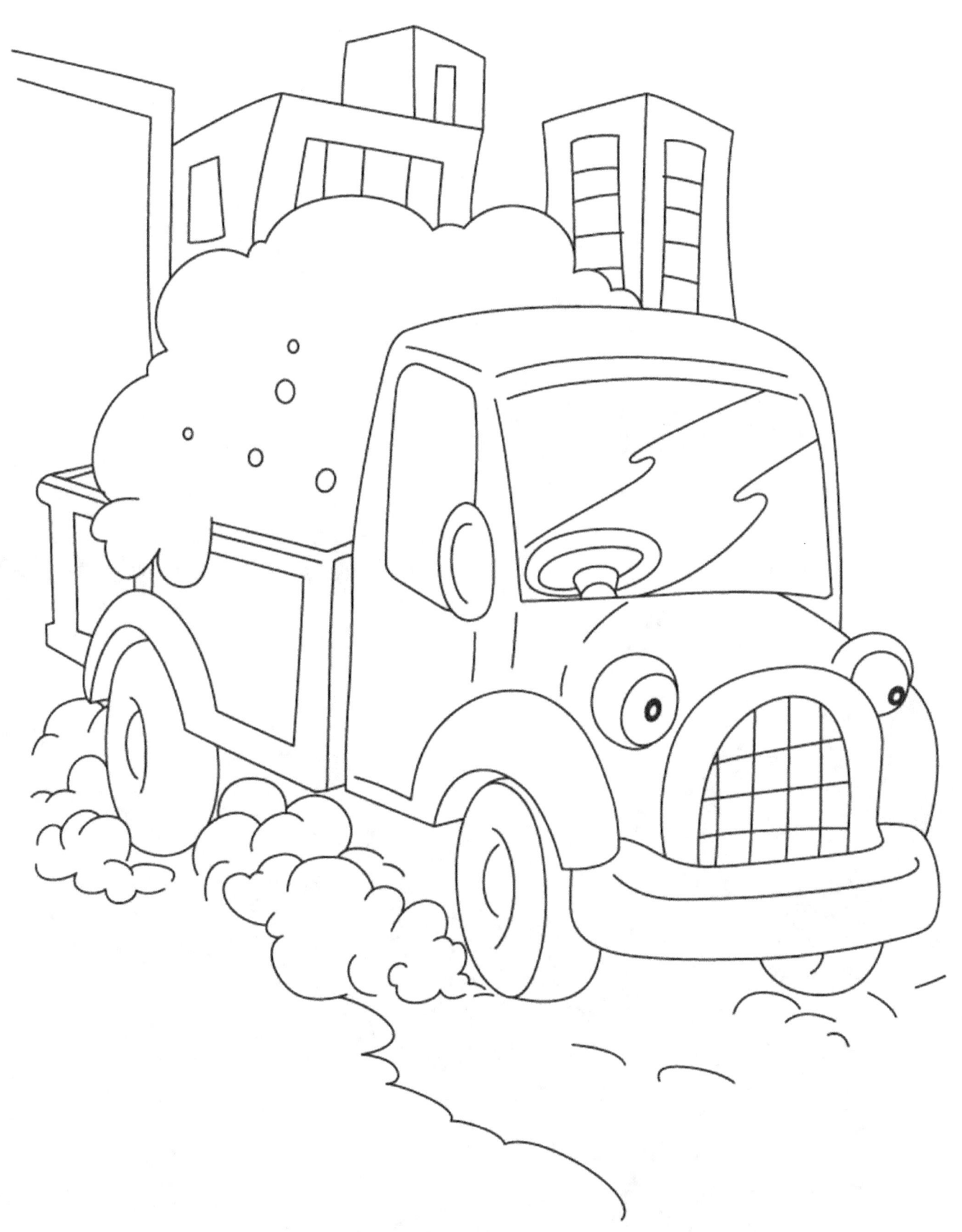

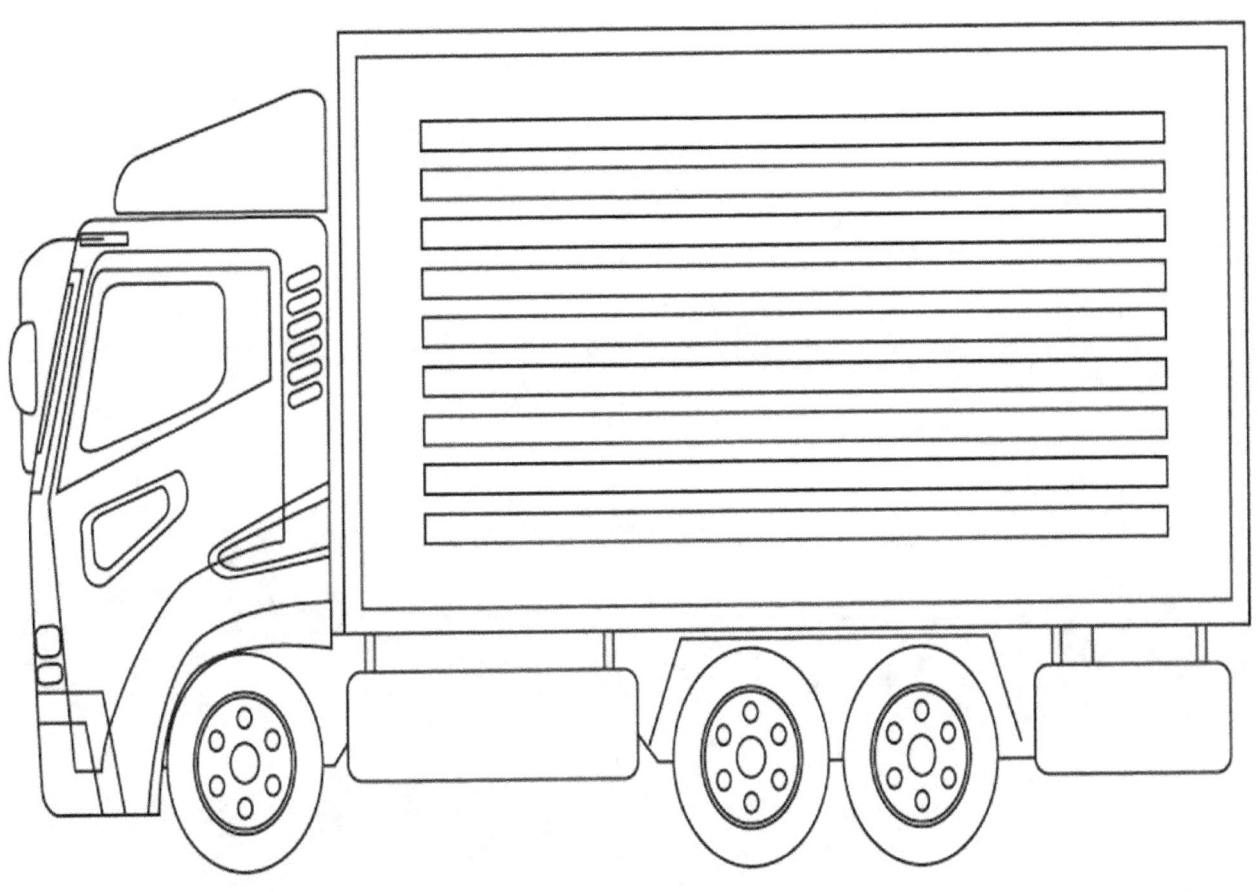

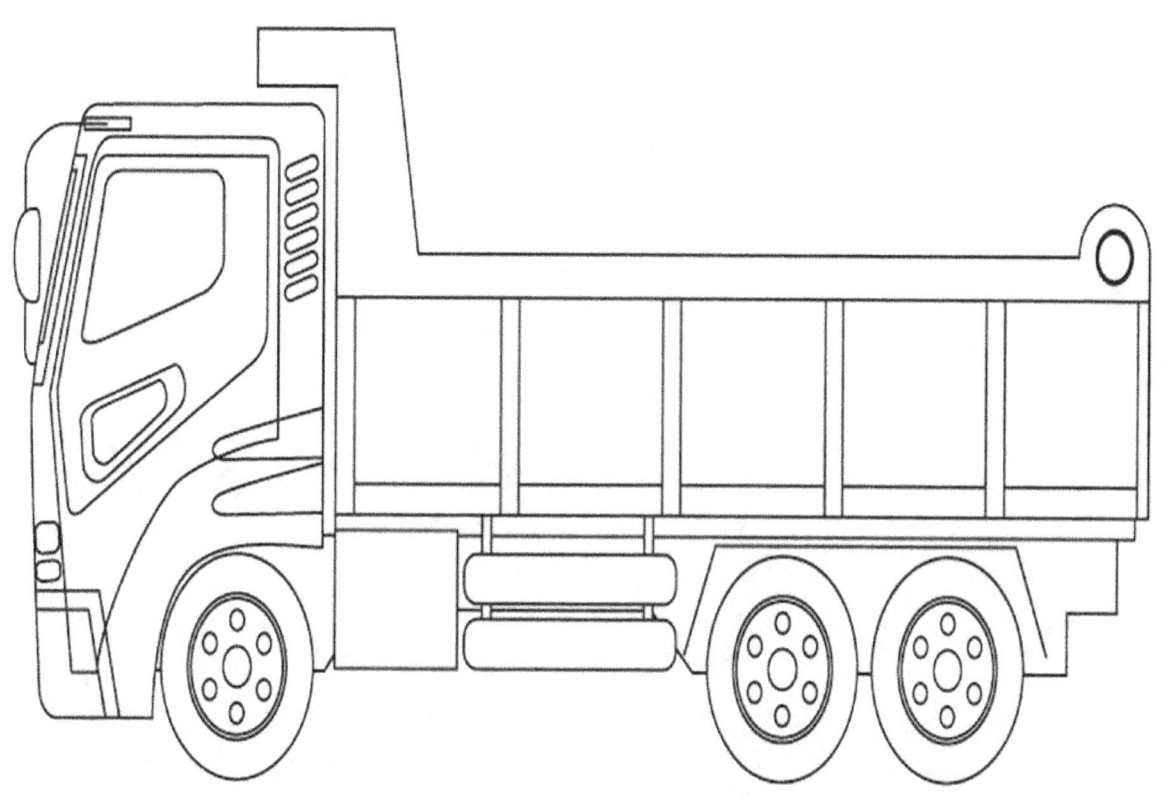

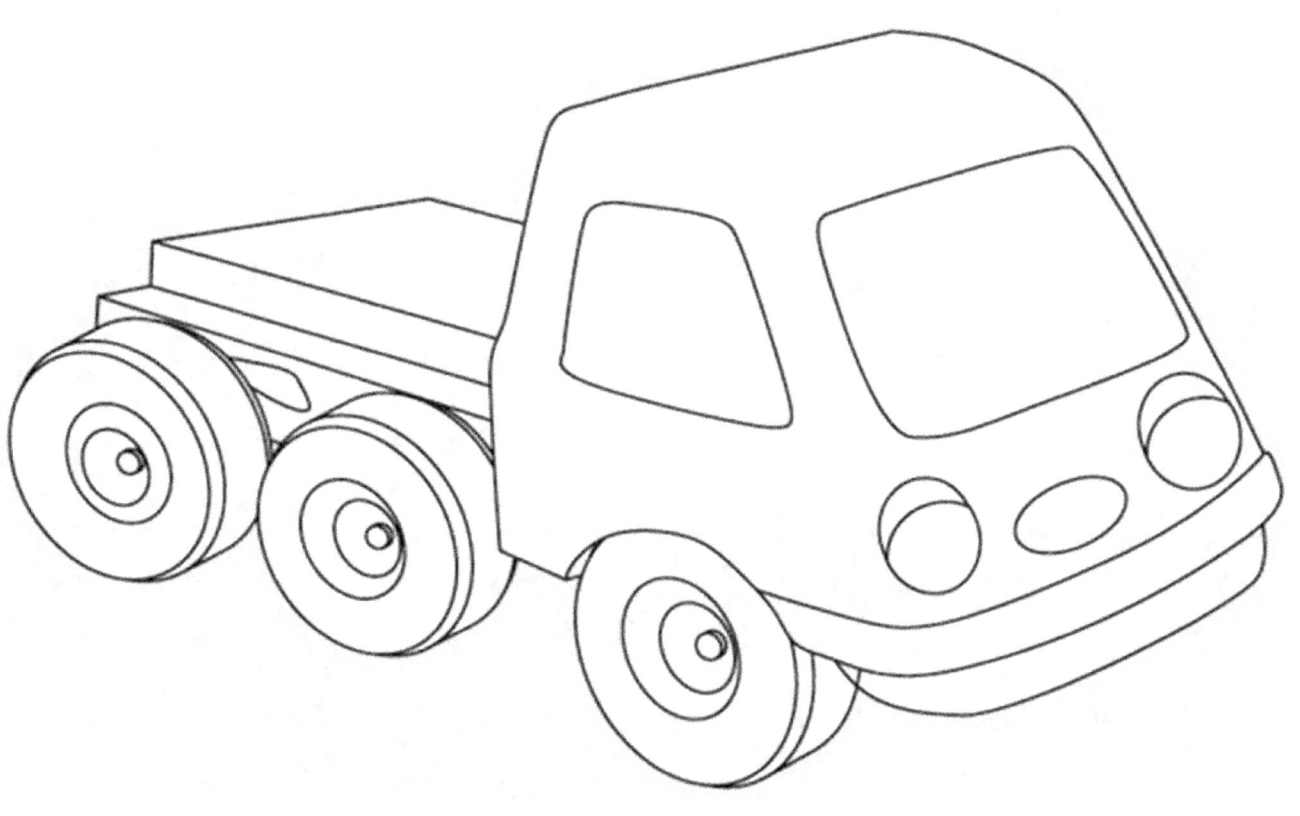

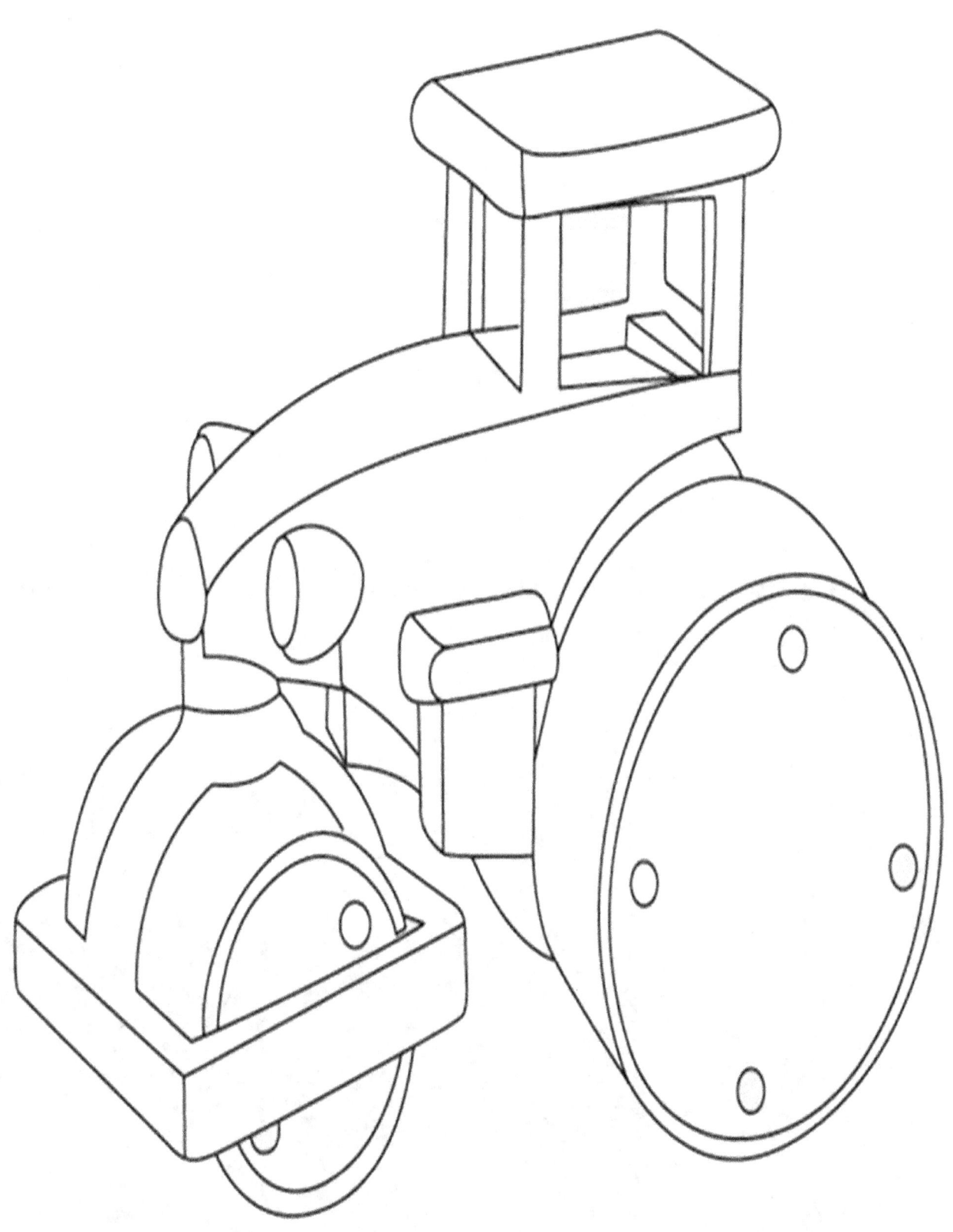

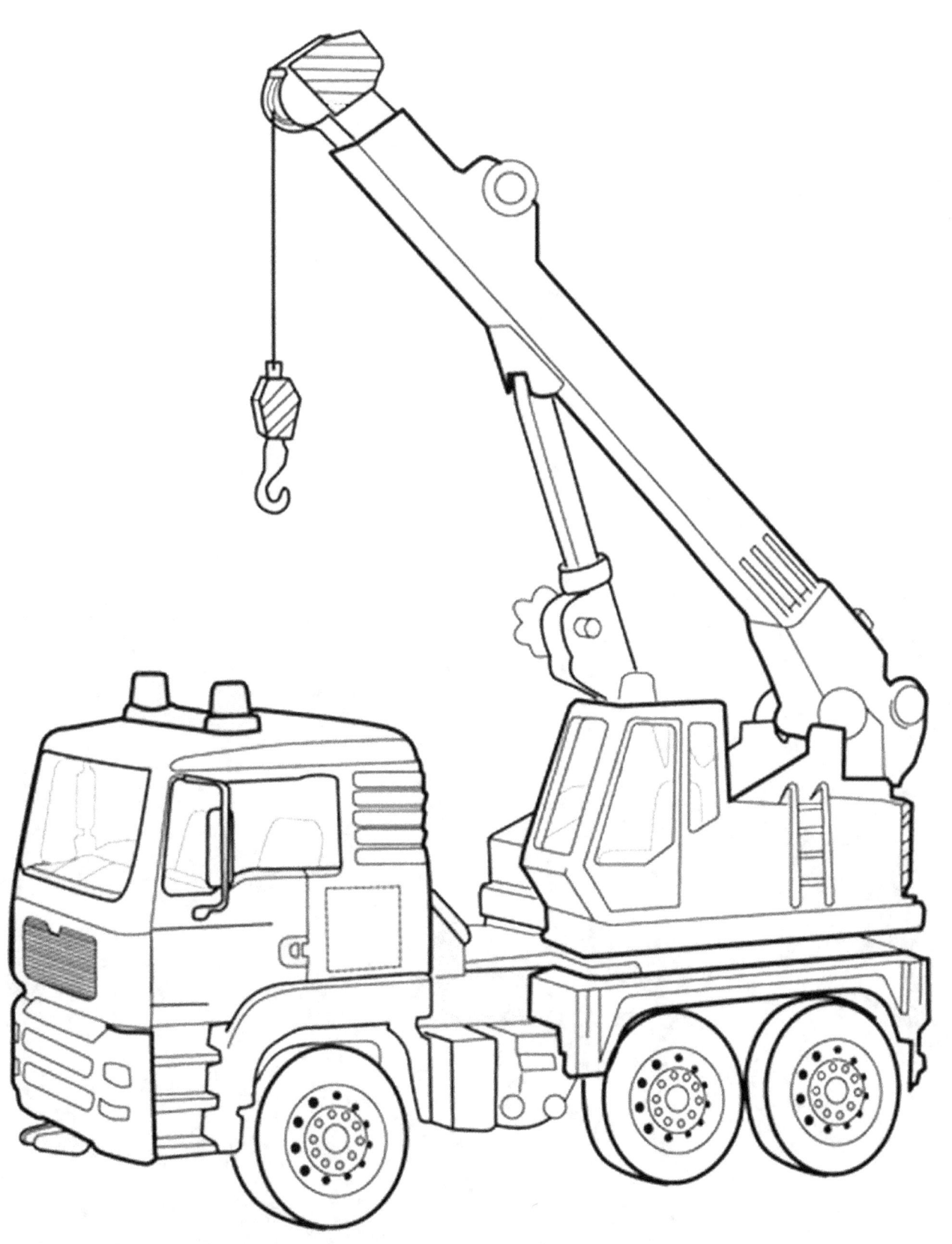

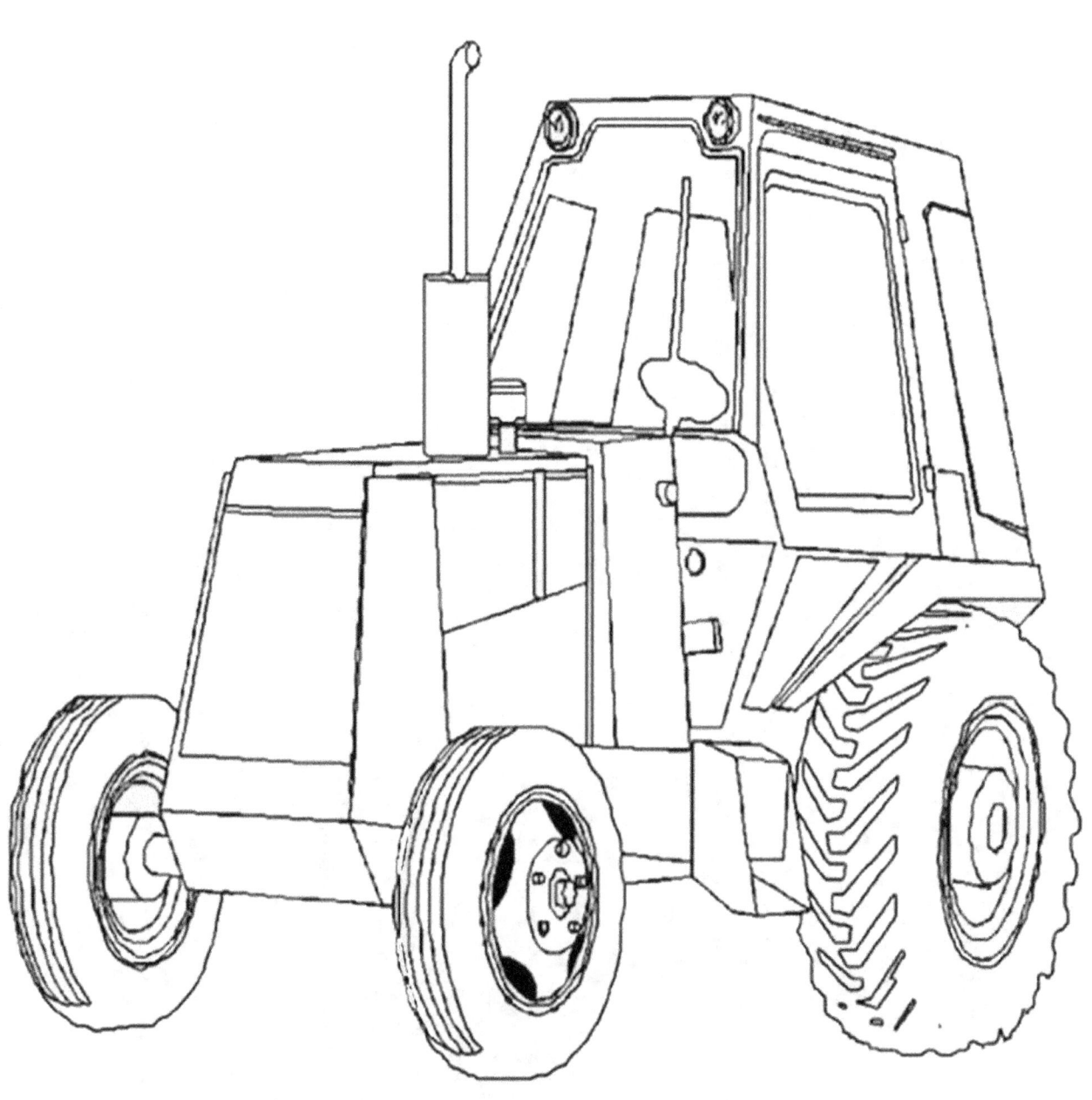

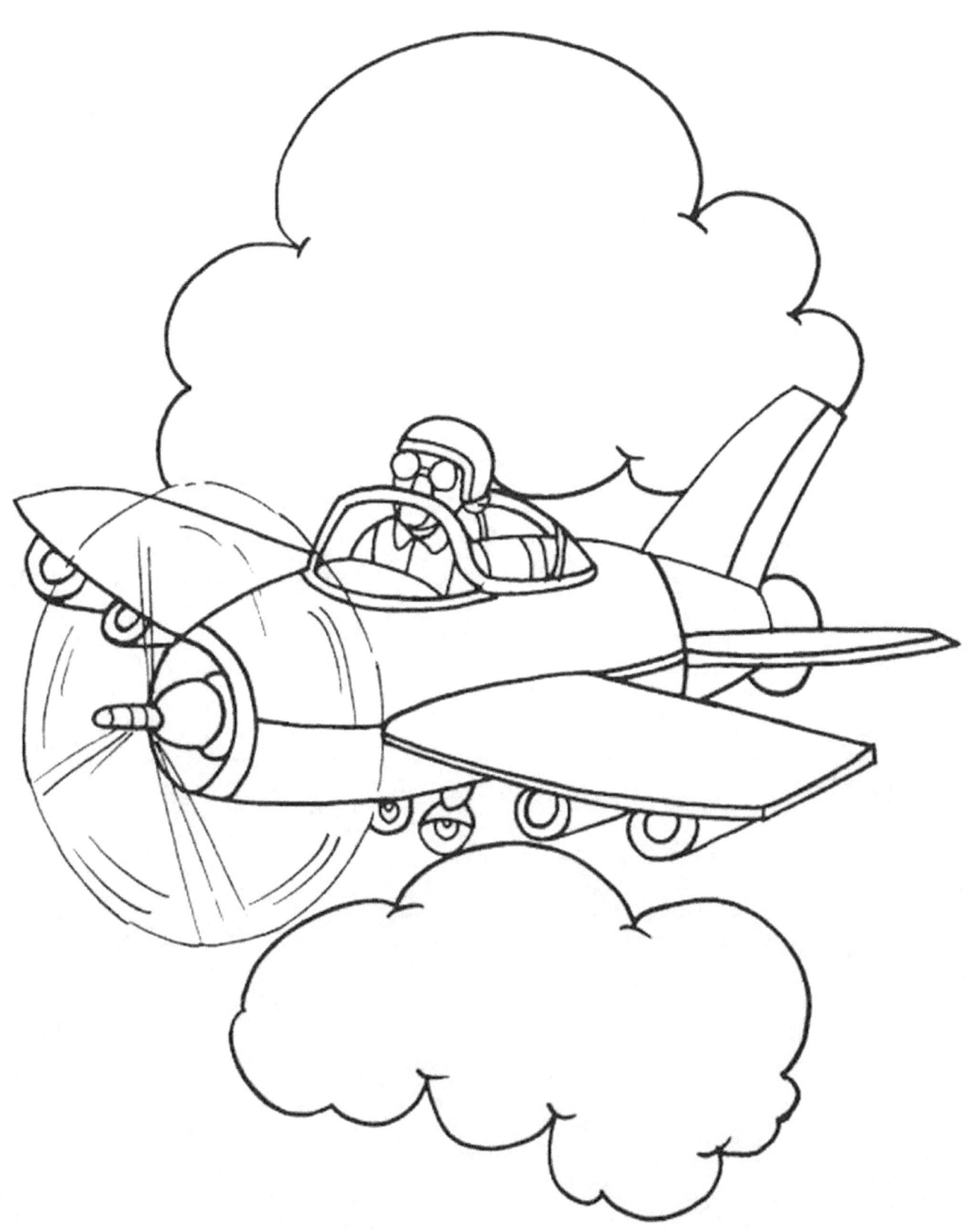

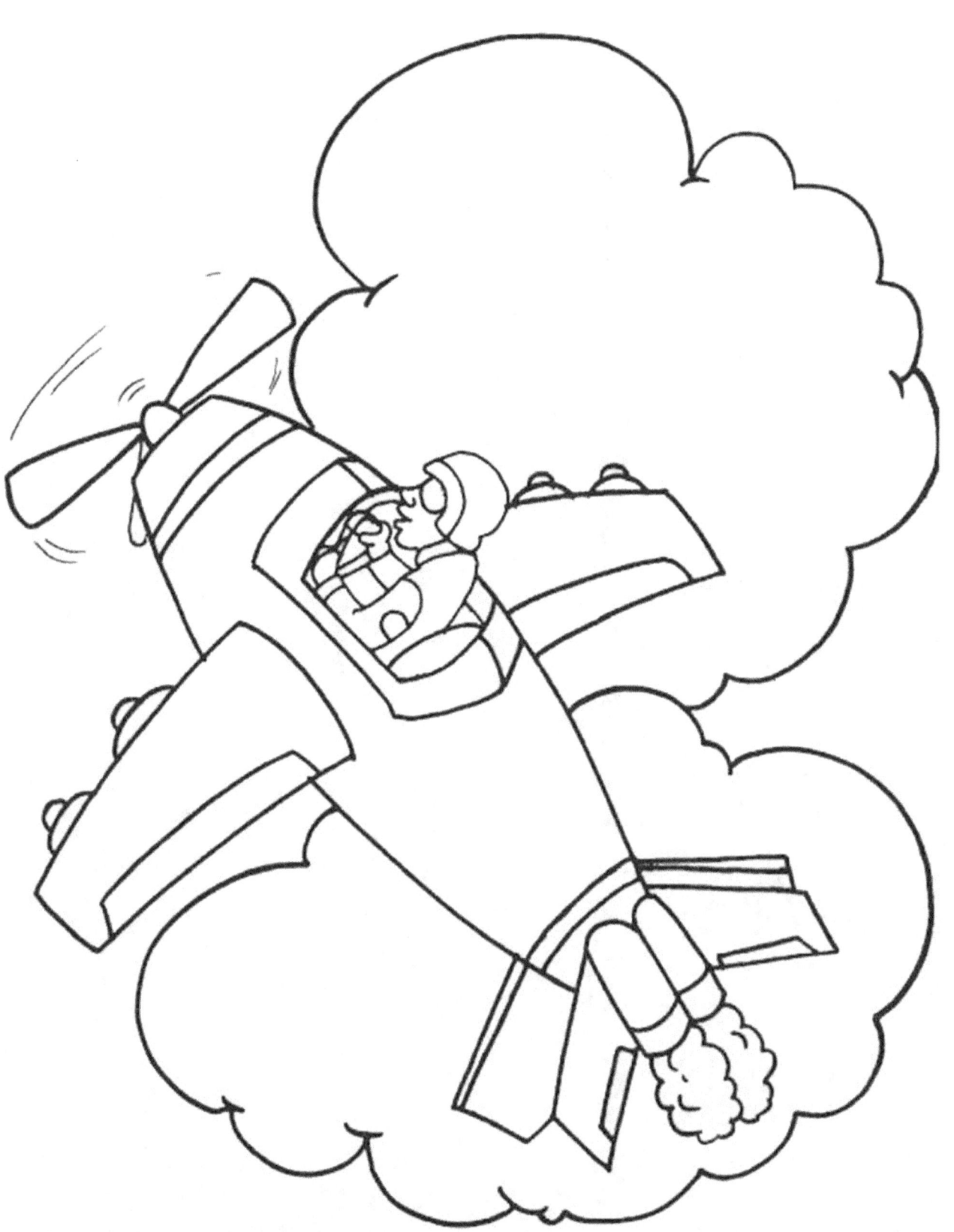

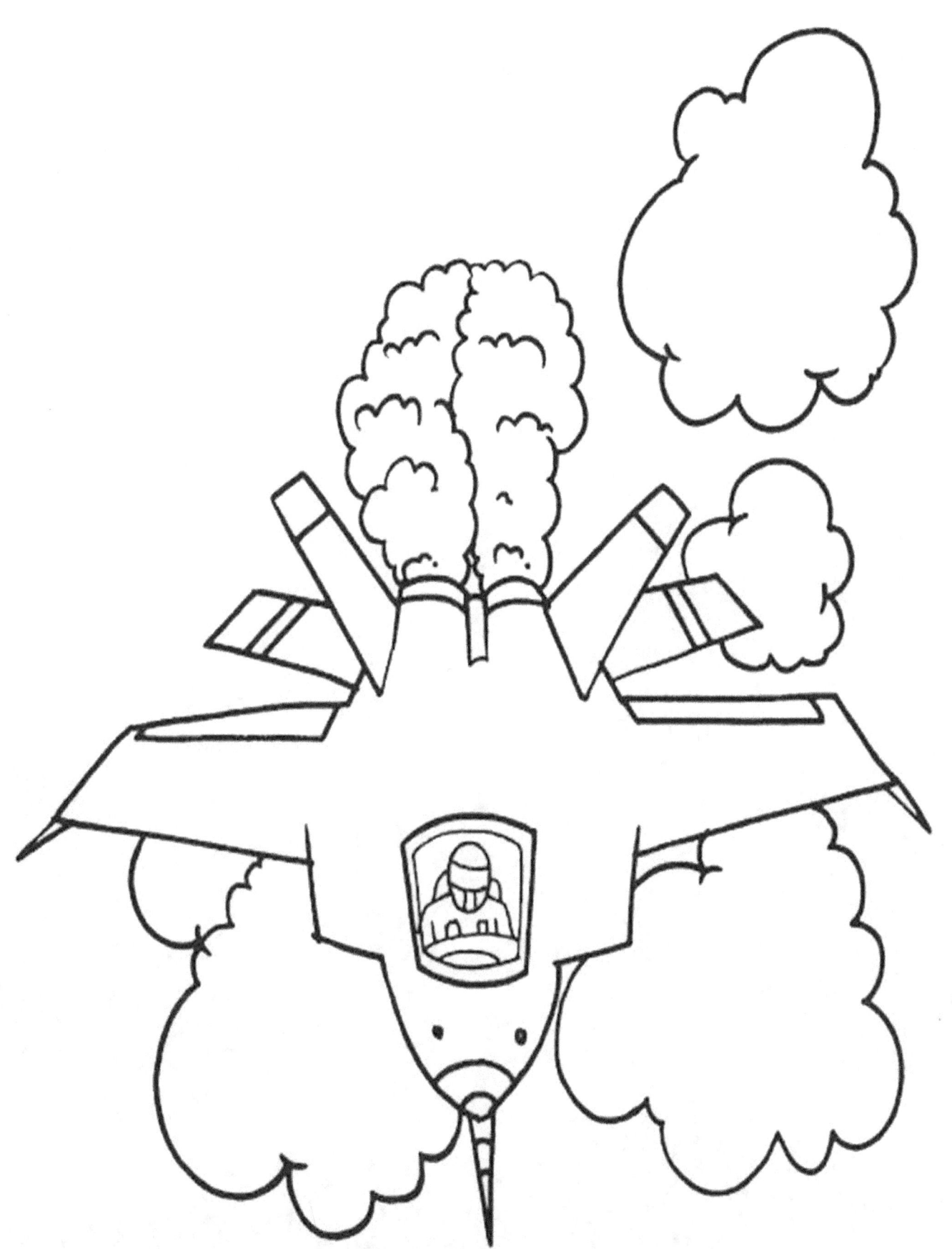

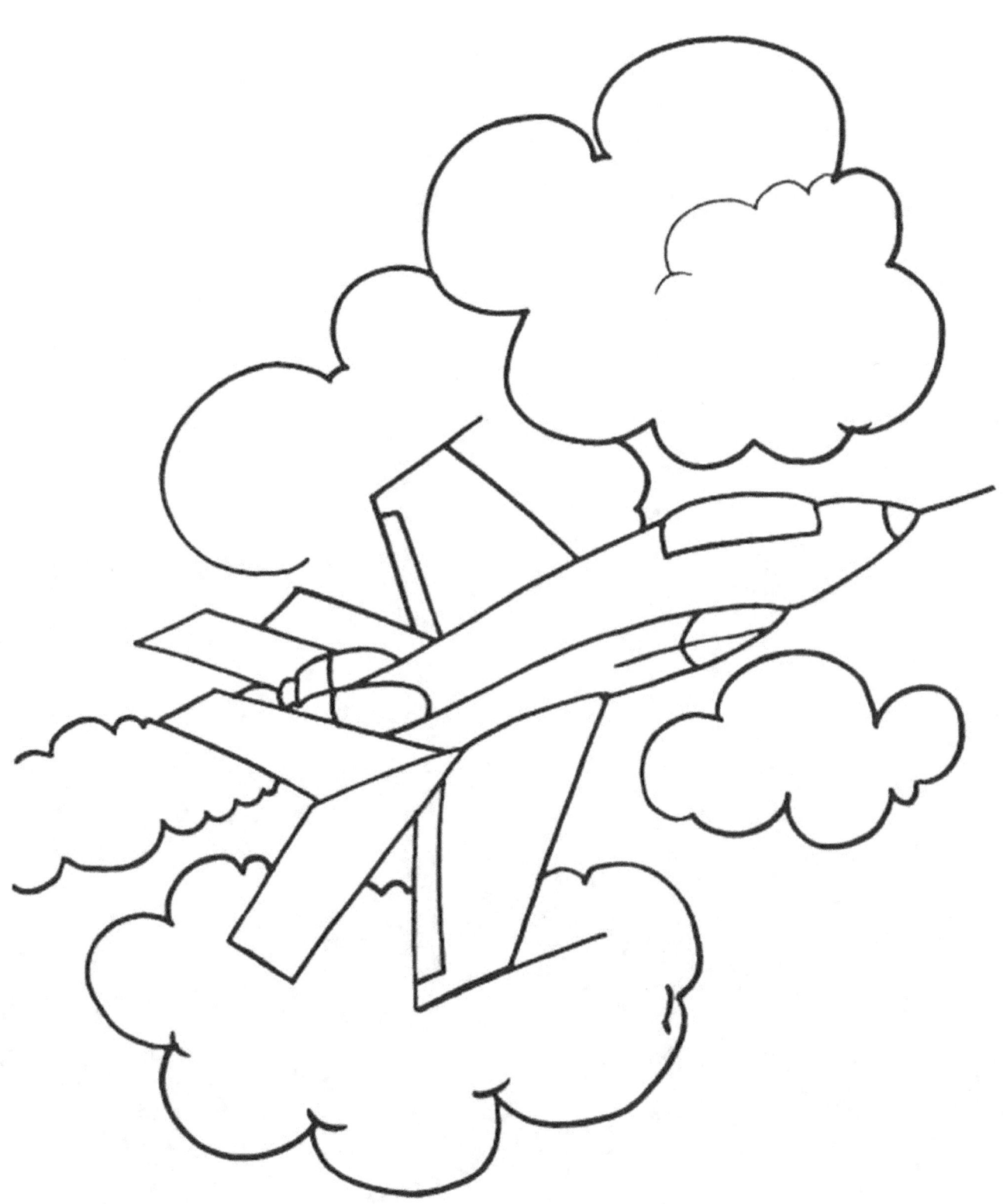

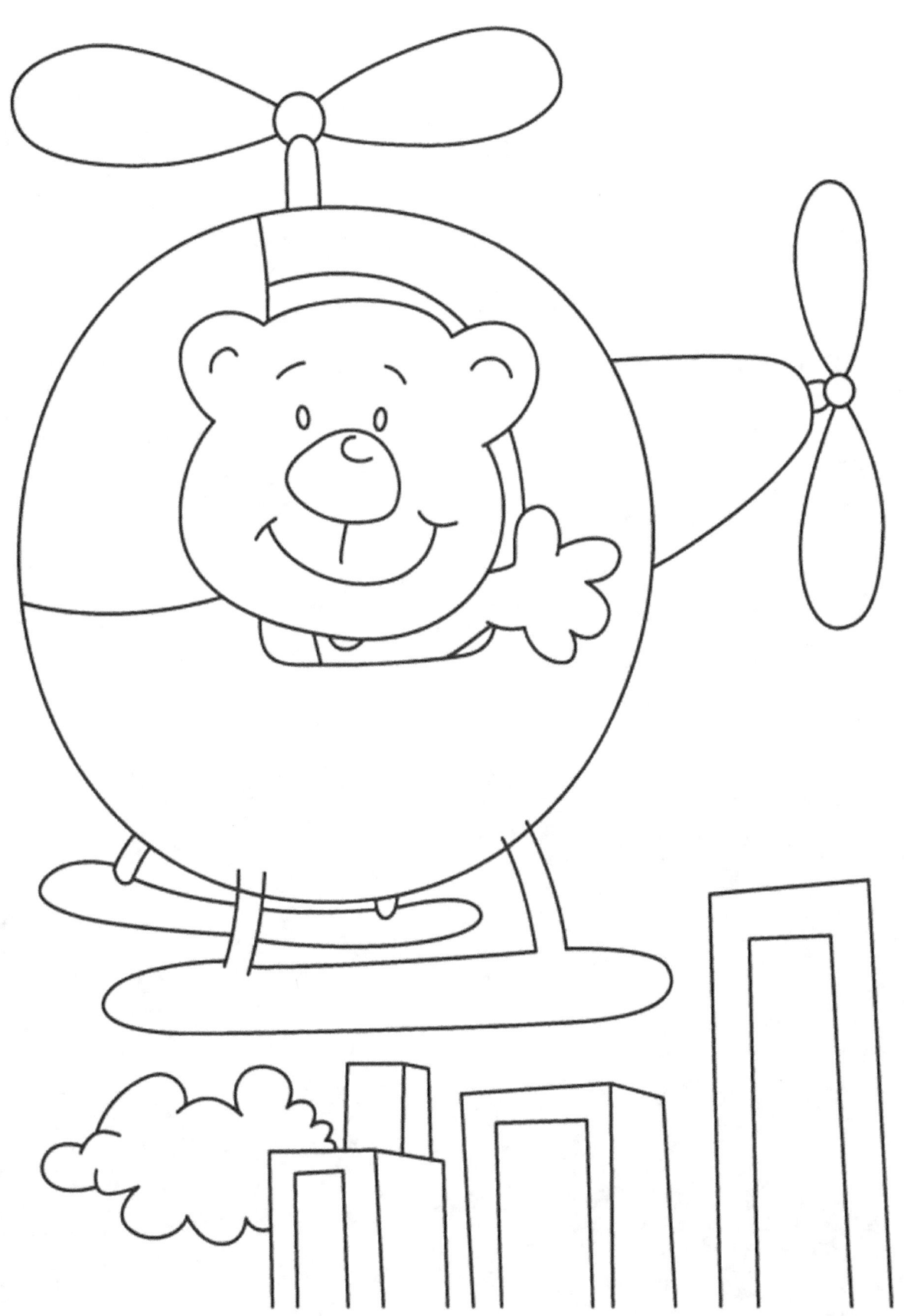

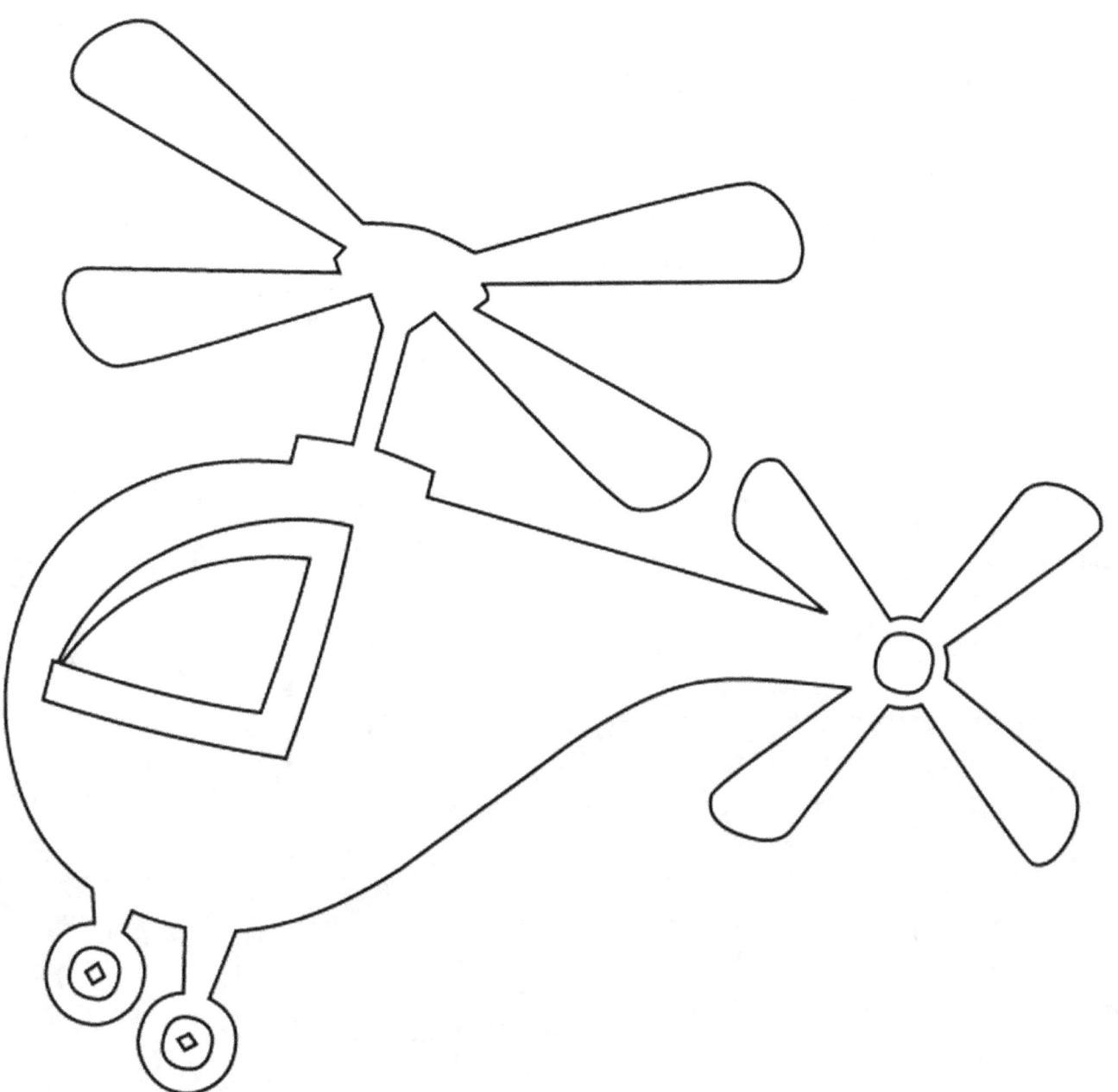

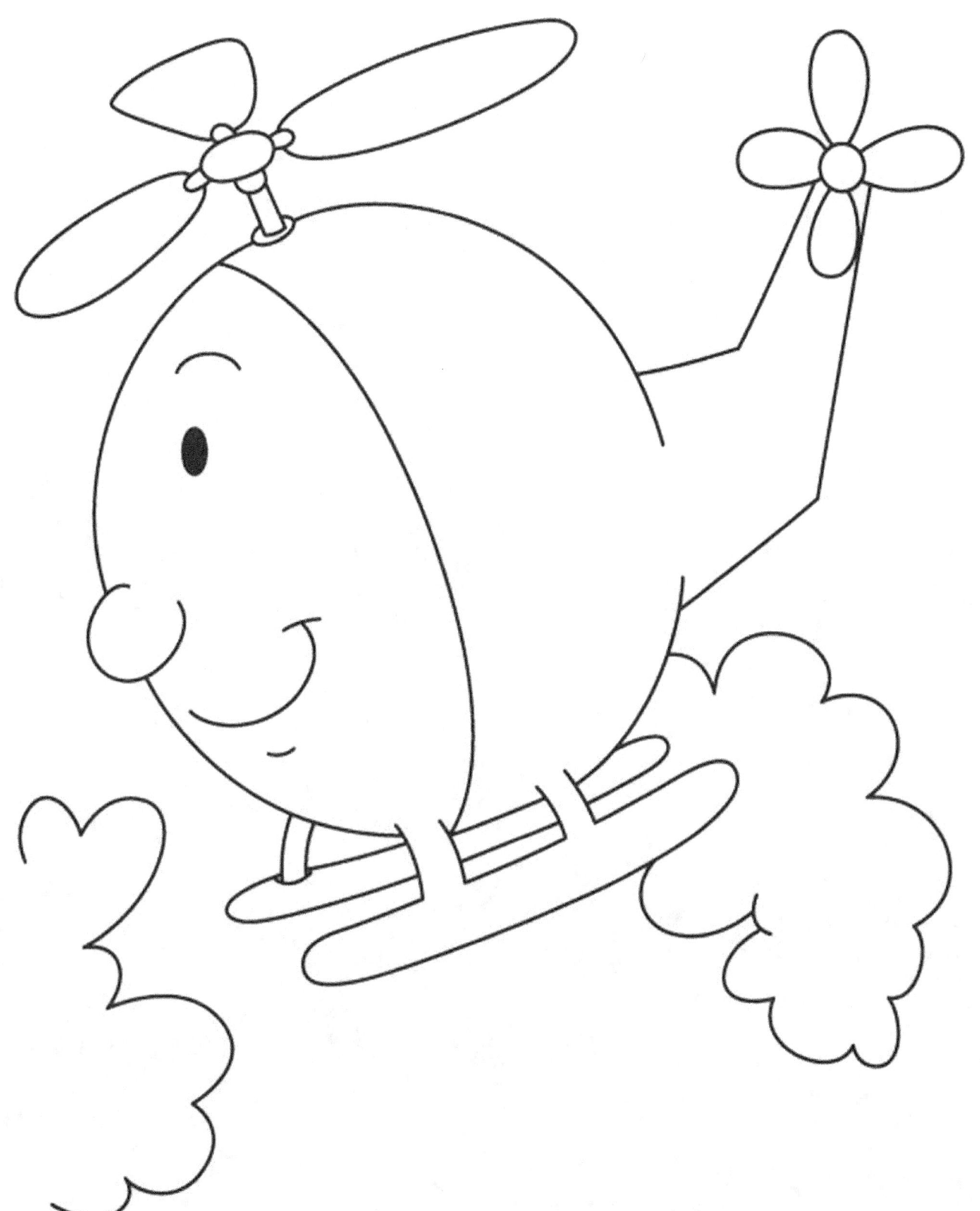

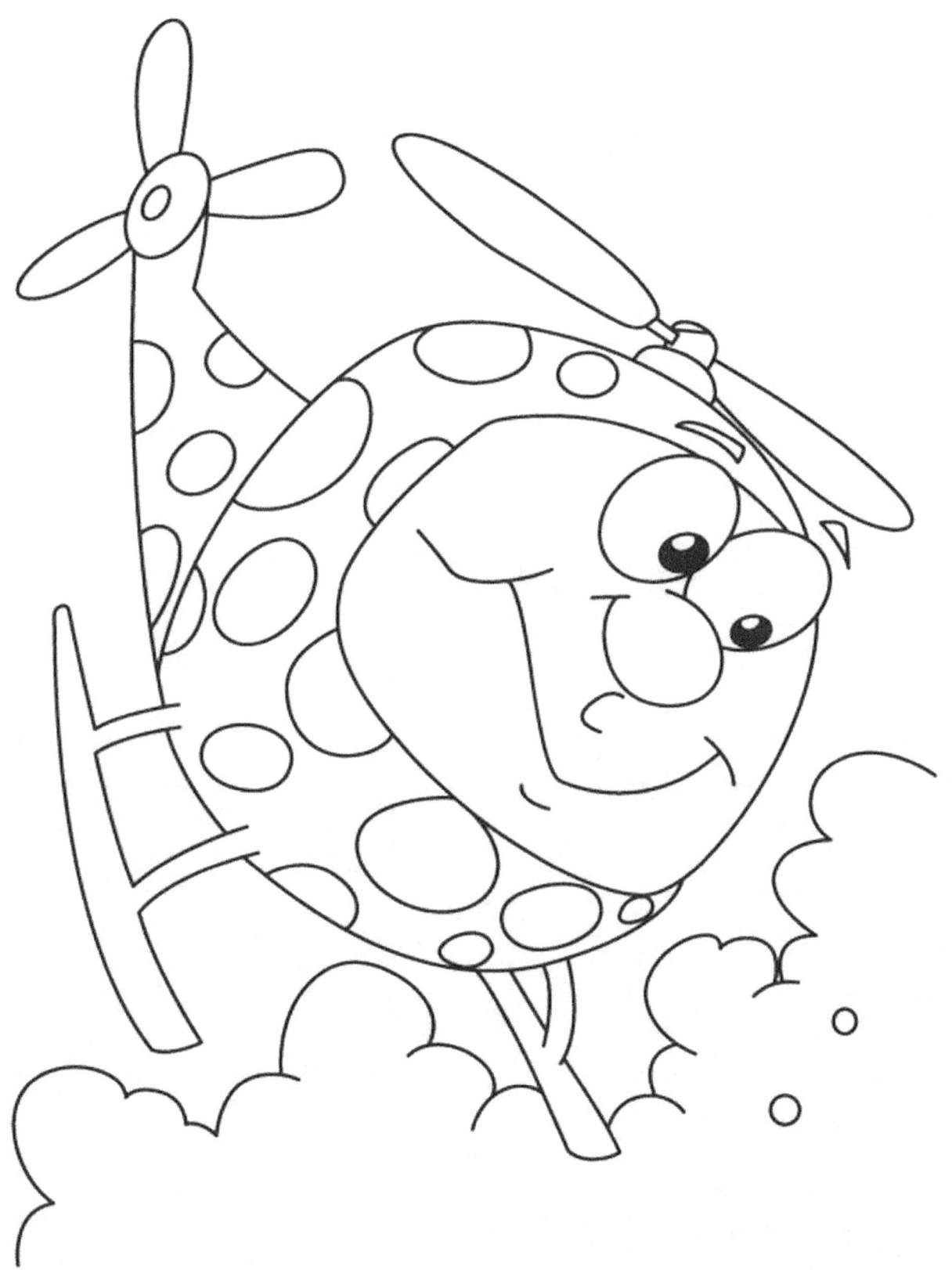

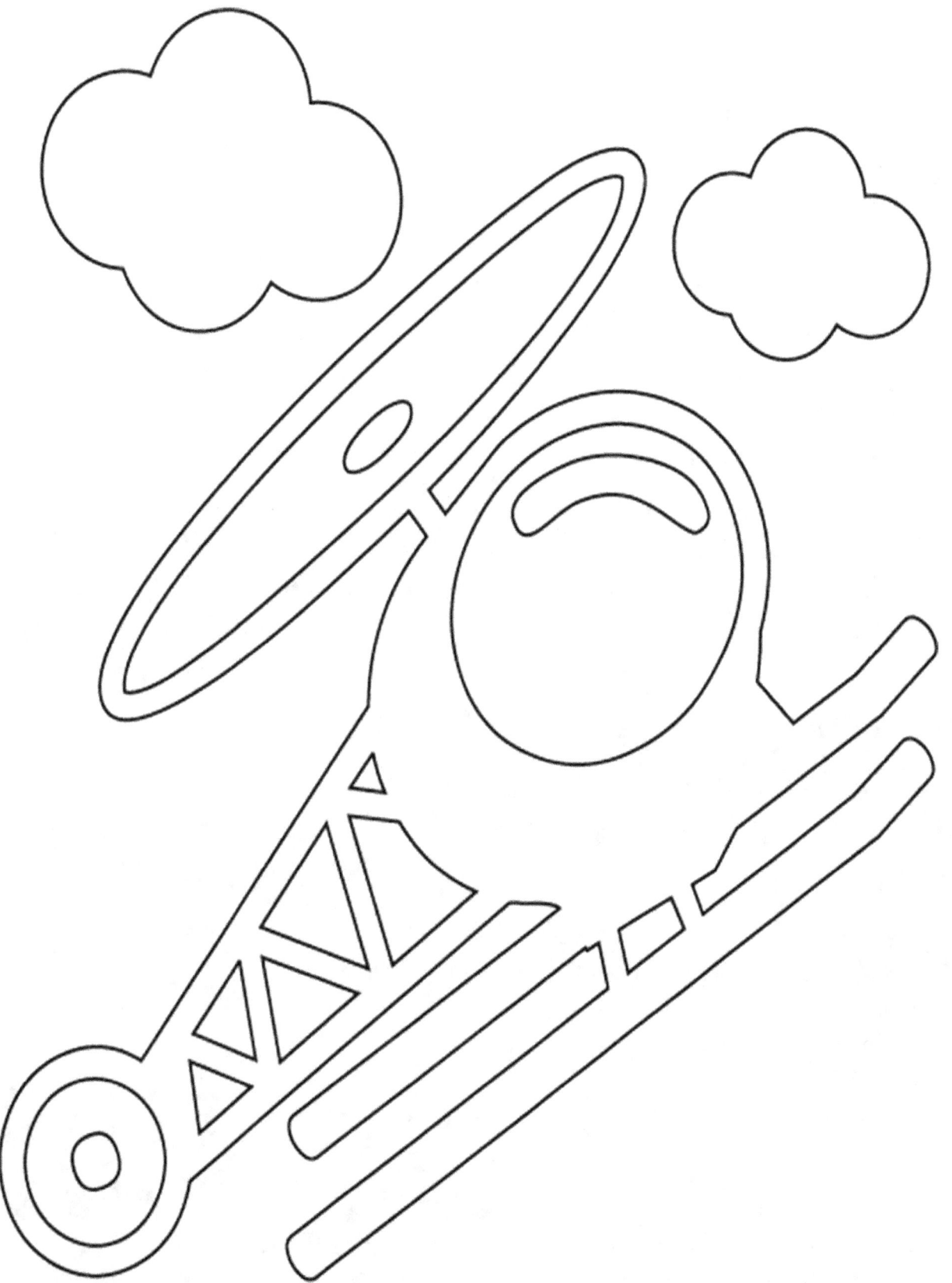

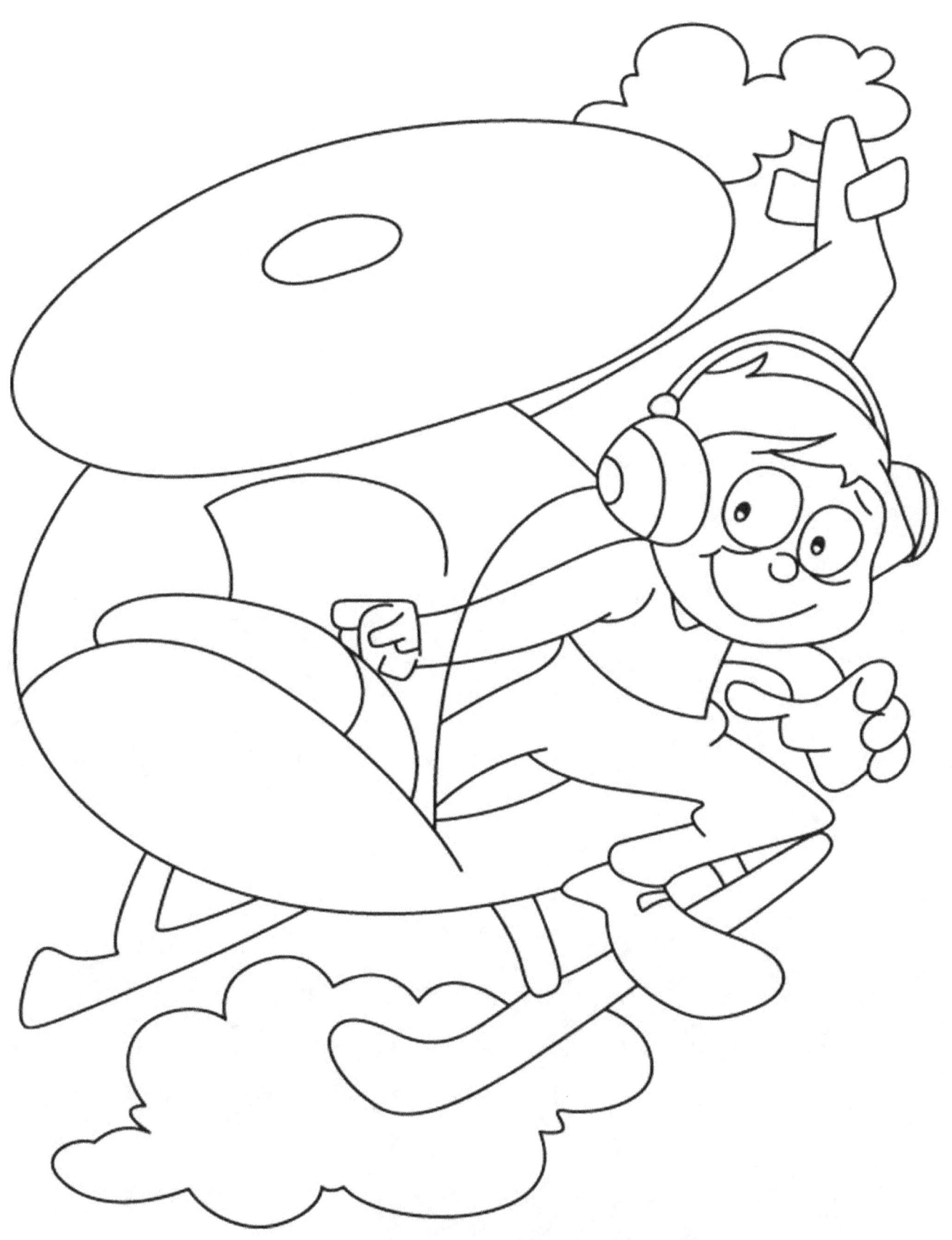

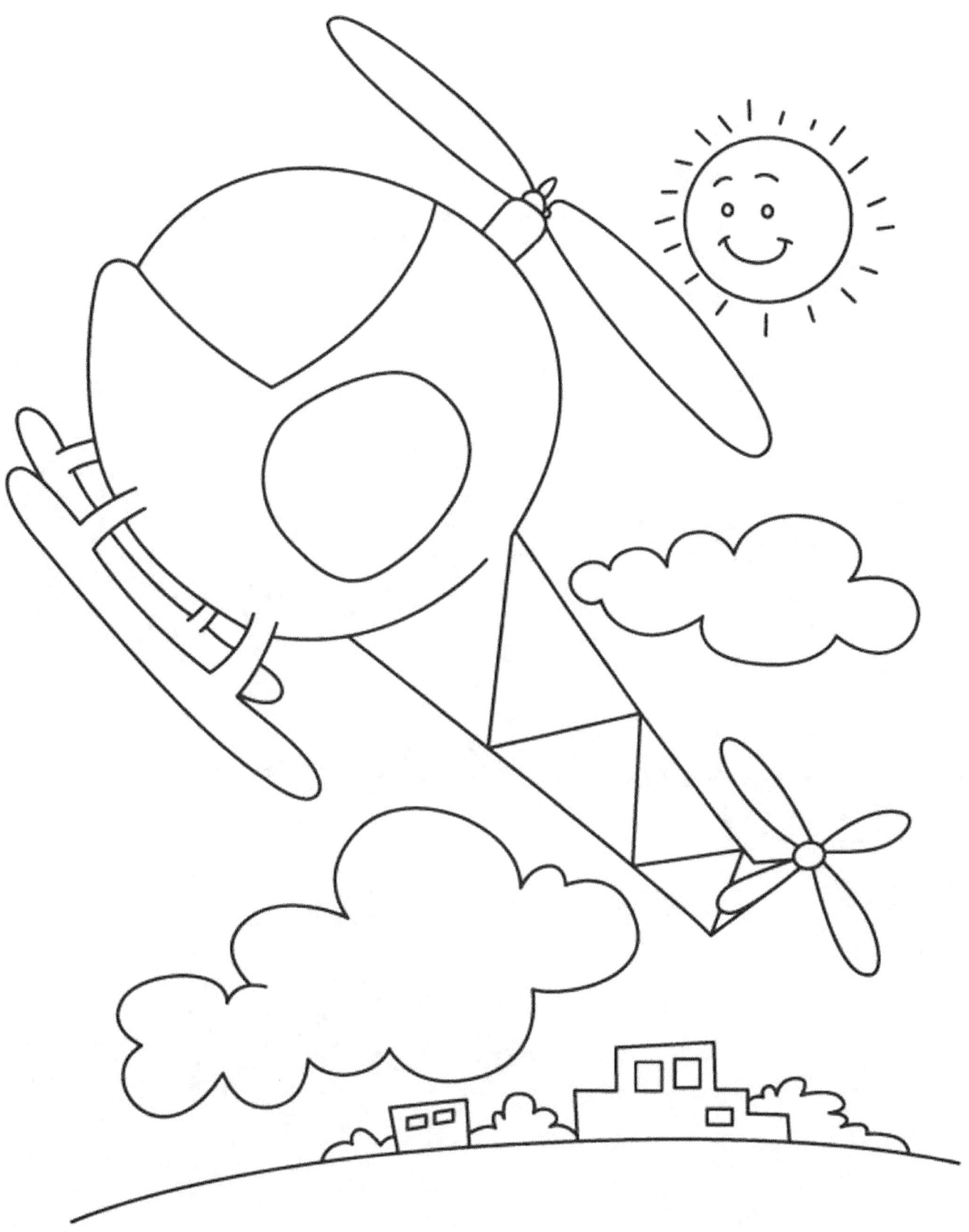

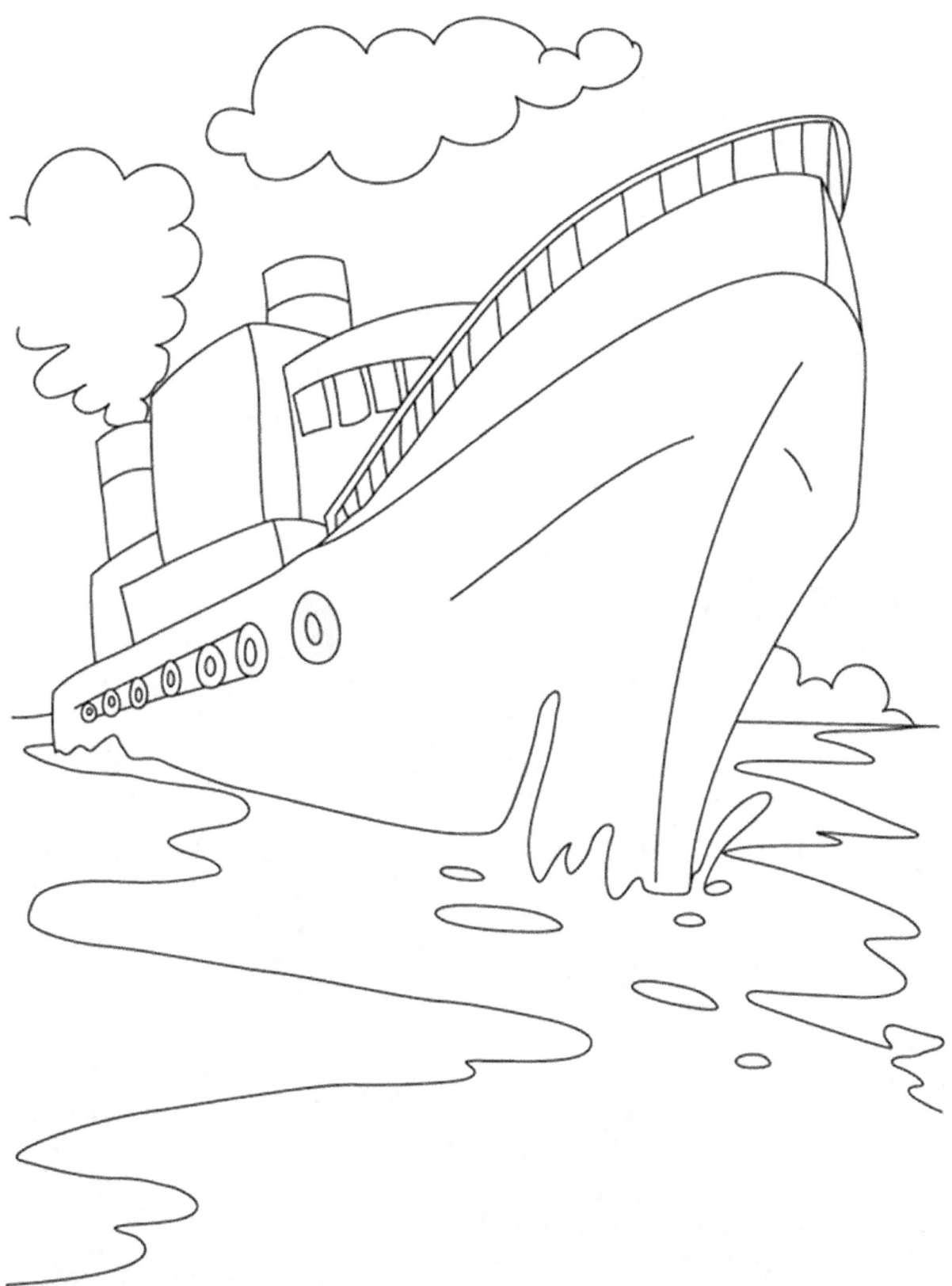

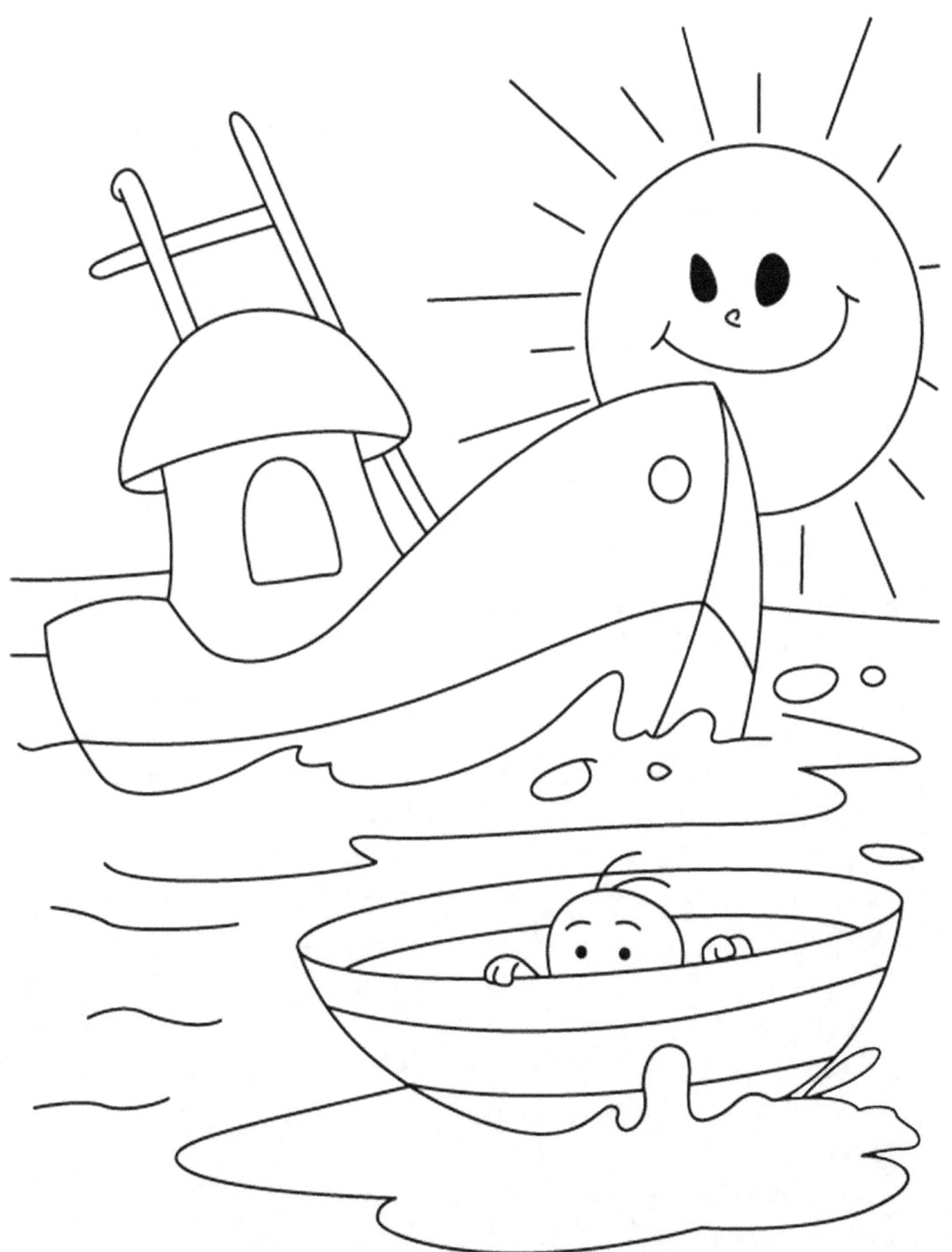

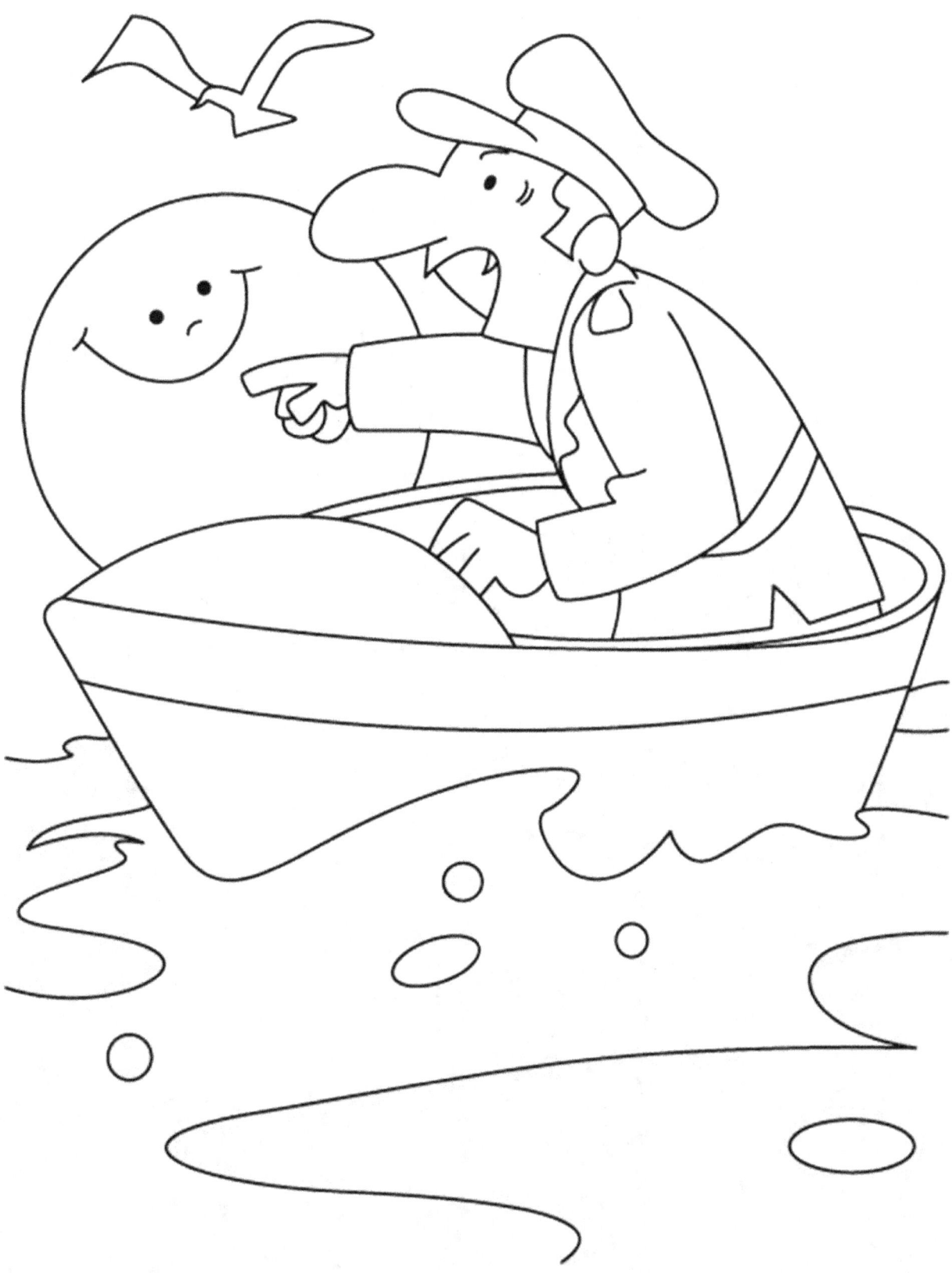

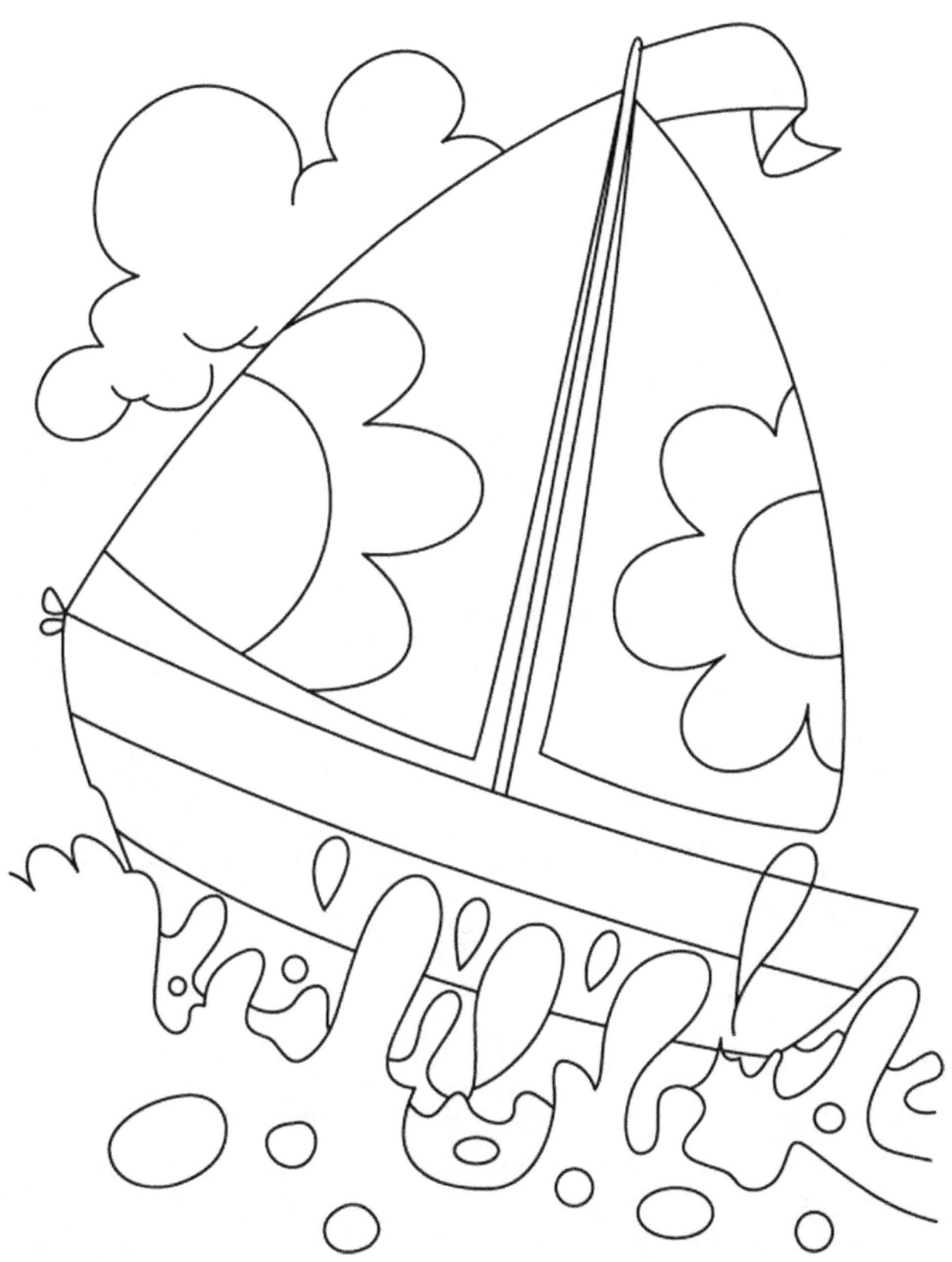

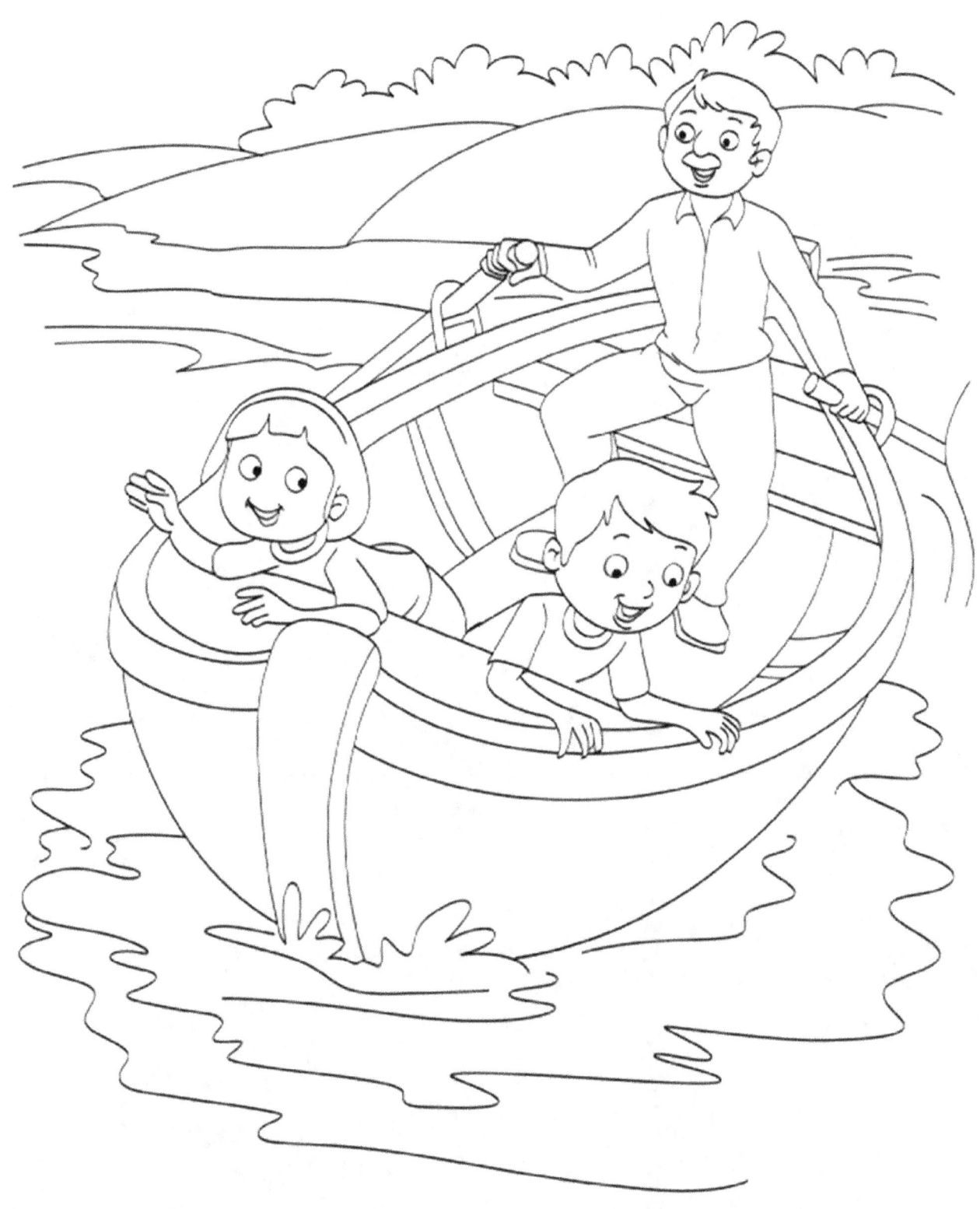

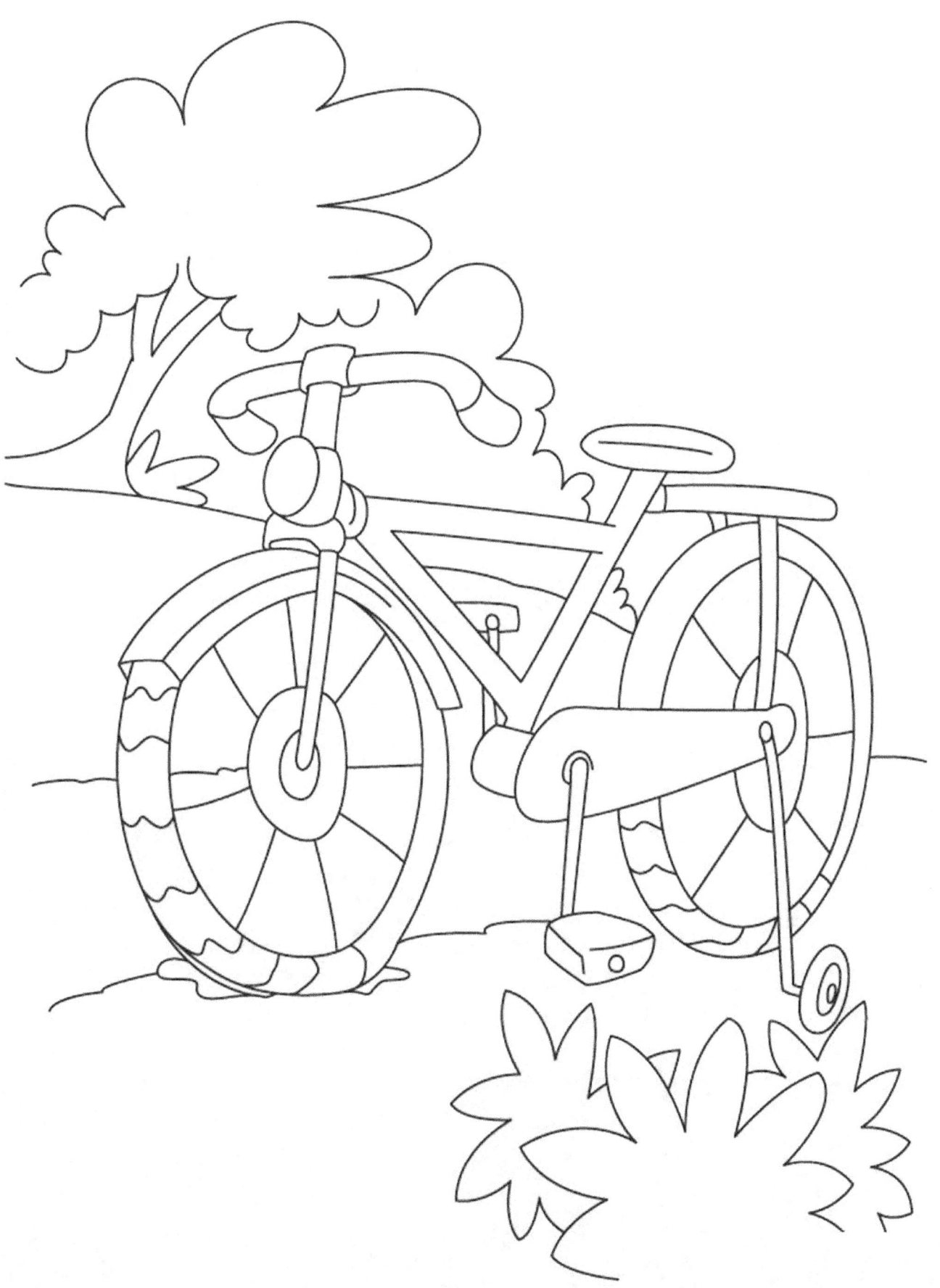

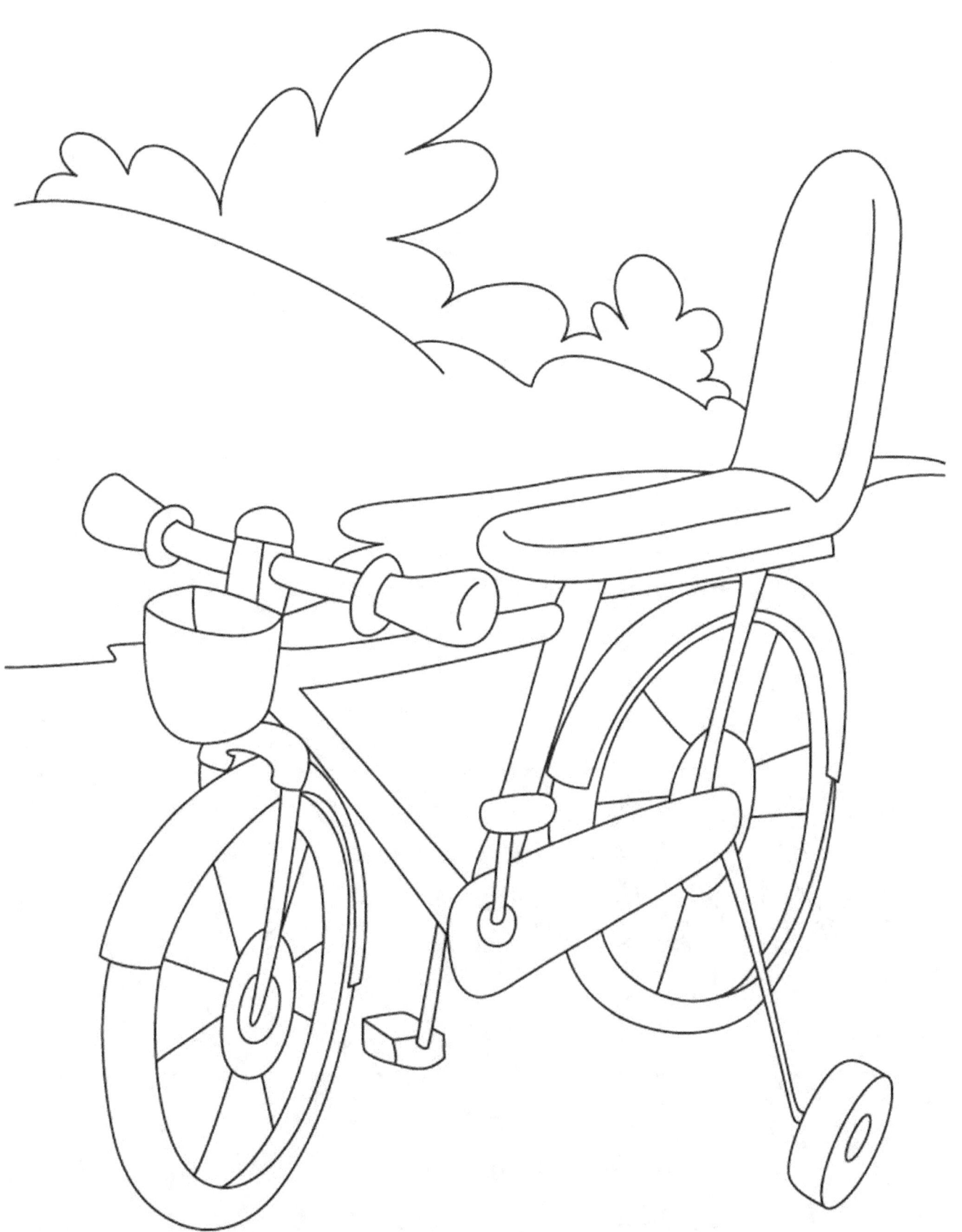

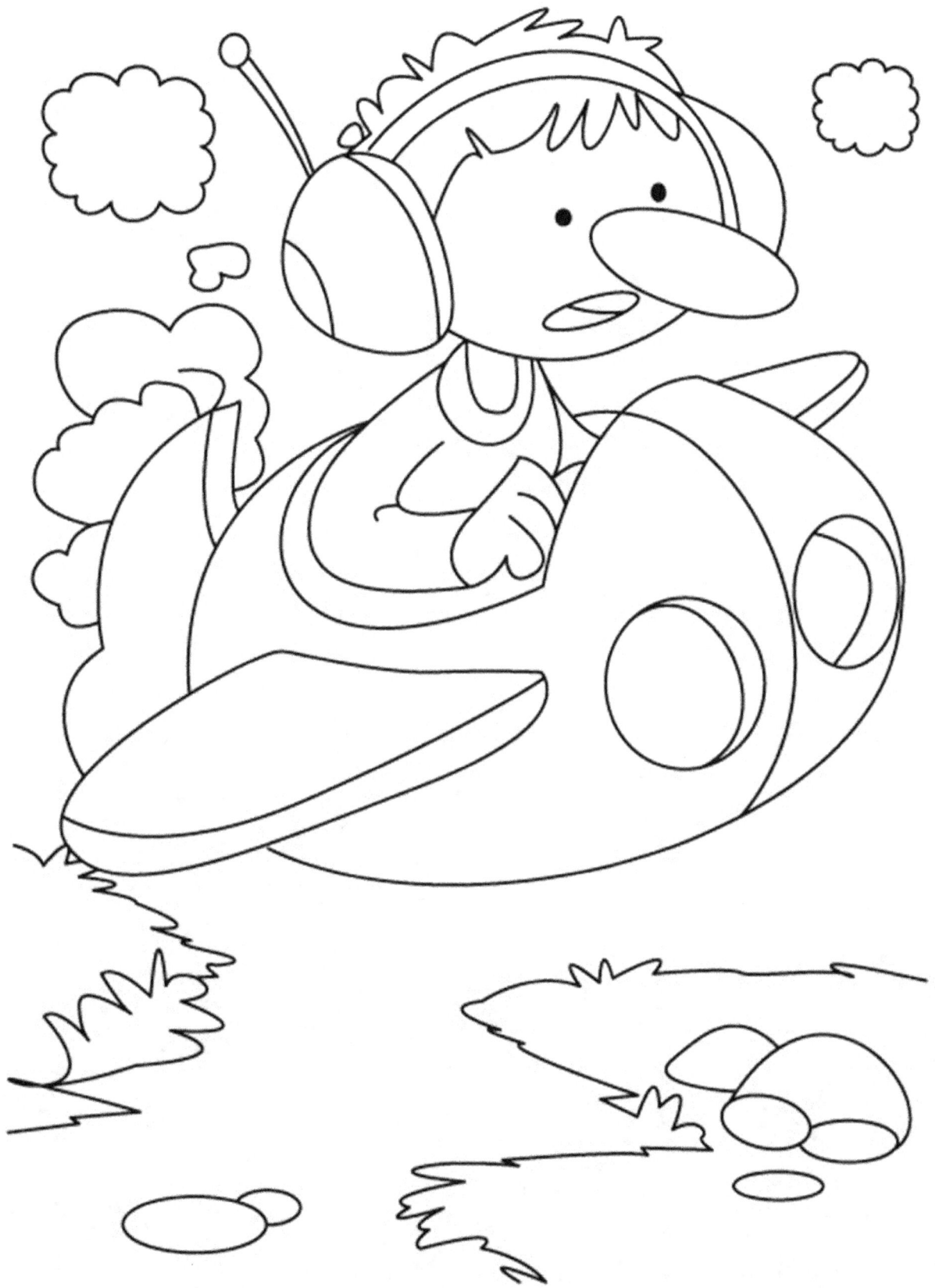

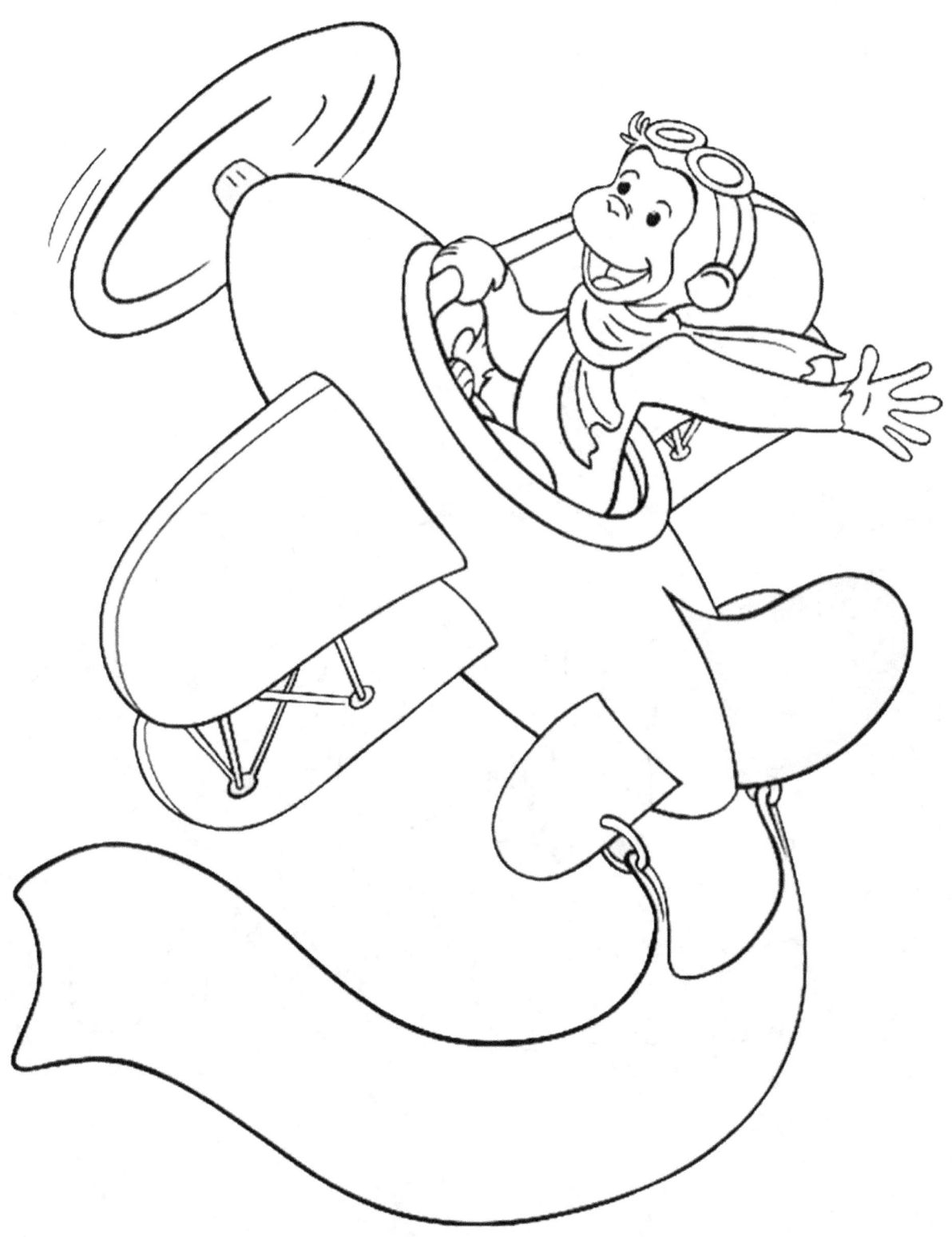

THANK YOU

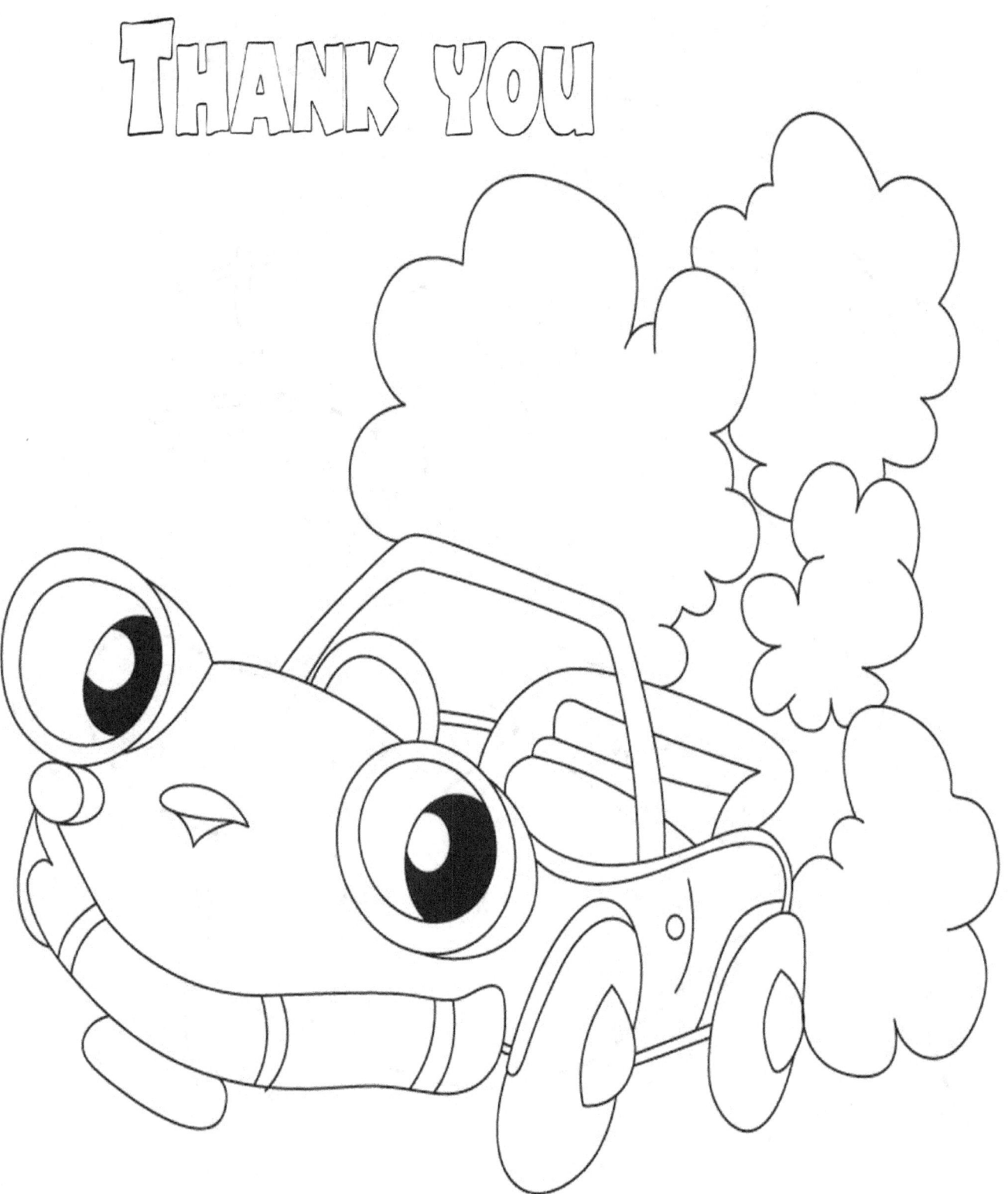